PR*A*

LONE OPERATOR

"Candid, enthralling, and brutally honest, Joseph Teti's *Lone Operator* shares actual events forged in life-changing trials which anyone can relate to. The intrinsic value of tough love and his warrior mindset enables our human spirit to survive and endure life's inevitable challenges."

—Michael S. Tucker, Lieutenant General US Army, (Ret.)
Former Commanding General First United States Army

"An elite spec ops commando, stockbroker and television star. For most of us, any one of the three would make for a fulfilling life—not for Joseph. *Lone Operator* tells the detailed, riveting true-life story of battlefield experiences defending the nation as well as his TV life as the star of Discovery Channel's *Dual Survival*, but most importantly, Joseph uses his many amazing life experiences to inspire us all to live our lives to the fullest."

—French Horwitz, Network Executive Producer, *Dual Survival*

"Riveting book about the journey of an American patriot that put his heart and soul in the defense of our great nation. Joseph explains how he has learned hard lessons in life, by combining thoughtfulness and simplicity, on how to not only to survive, but to thrive in today's ever changing complex world."

—Rion Choate, Investment Banker, Harvard Business School, Senior Fellow at the John F. Kennedy School of Government

Lone Operator:
A Survival Manual for the Modern Age

by Joseph N. Teti with Liam Wolfe

ISBN 978-1-63393-979-0

Published by

◤ köehlerbooks™

210 60th Street
Virginia Beach, VA 23451
800-435-4811
www.koehlerbooks.com

LONE OPERATOR

HOW TO SURVIVE & THRIVE IN THE MODERN AGE

JOSEPH N. TETI

WITH LIAM WOLFE

VIRGINIA BEACH
CAPE CHARLES

AUTHOR'S NOTE

HAVING SERVED MY COUNTRY in the unique capacities that I have in both military and government special operations, I wanted to ensure that I did not compromise any operational security, information, or TTPs (Tactics, Techniques, and Procedures). I am morally, ethically, and legally obligated to protect such sensitive information, not including declassified and open source information found on the Internet. I have purposely used false names, dates, places, and times to protect sensitive information. This book is based on true events.

DEDICATION

IT IS SAID THAT if you are blessed with that one special person that changes you for the better, you are very lucky. I have known many people, but one in particular has been a constant motivation for me to live the best that I can and to understand that tomorrow is not promised, but a gift. Mike Donatelli was a dear friend who made such an impact on my life. I find it only fitting to give him the credit he is due. It would take pages for me to chronicle all the memories I have of this incredible man. One of my fondest was my early morning phone call. Every day he would call me at six in the morning, his bolstering voice saying, "Wake up, Skippy, time to go to the gym." I was usually just getting up and showering—not Mike. He was either done working out at the boxing gym or just pulling into the parking lot, long enough to stick his boot up my ass to get my day going. He was a highly motivated and disciplined individual, even by special operations standards. A meticulous planner, I learned many things from him when it came to figuring out solutions to my day-to-day problems.

Even more impressive and a credit to his character was his ability to stay the course, and as he would put it, "stick to the high ground." He was referencing maintaining my moral high ground. His ability to always see the best in all things and never have a bad word for someone, even when they deserved it, was a feat that I have not seen in anyone but him. As God is my witness, if I can be half the man Mike was, I will have considered my life one that was well lived. His death has been difficult to bear. But with the pain of such a loss, I have gained a new perspective that has made me a better person.

MSG (R) Michael W. Donatelli
1967-2013
Ranger, Green Beret, Delta Force

TABLE OF CONTENTS

Introduction. 1

Part 1: War Stories—My Life under Fire 3

Chapter One—The Will to Win: *The Boar Story*. 5

Chapter Two—The Final Option: *Seventy-seven Hours*. 15

Chapter Three—The Warrior Mindset: *I'm Hit!*. 29

Chapter Four—Planning for the Worst: *The Helo Crash*. 42

Chapter Five—Crawl, Walk, Run: *The Making of
a Commando (Part 1)*. 54

Chapter Six—No More Wooden Guns: *The Making of
a Commando (Part 2)*. 67

Chapter Seven—Out of School: *And into the Fire* 84

Chapter Eight—The Tao of Capitalism: *Or How to Fail
at Business without Really Trying*. 98

Chapter Nine—Fight or Flight: *A Tale of South Africa* 111

Part 2: Survival—A Modern Manual. 141

Chapter Ten—Joe's Top Ten Rules for Startups 143

Chapter Eleven—Ten Rules for Surviving and
Thriving in the Modern World. 152

Chapter Twelve—Relationship Survival:
The Four Pillars. 171

Chapter Thirteen—The Warrior Mindset:
Prepare for War 179

Epilogue—The Final Assessment: *Exfil*. 196

INTRODUCTION

TO BE PERFECTLY HONEST, I was not going to write an introduction, as I never read them when I buy a book. However, I will keep this short and sweet.

I wrote *Lone Operator* for several reasons. First and foremost, I would like to think I have led a rather unique life. I have had experiences that a person, if they were so inclined, could use to improve or quantify their own. I have known more than a few people that have passed away that lived amazing lives, only to take all their knowledge and experience to the grave. I find that tragically sad. I did not want to make the same mistake. By no means do I expect you to use or implement all the ideas and knowledge I have chronicled in this book. However, if you are like me and look for those priceless "gold nuggets" of information that you stumble across every now and then, I am sure you will not be disappointed when you finish reading this book.

I did not write this for notoriety or fame. After spending three years on *Dual Survival* on the Discovery Channel, I had more than enough of that to last the rest of my life. To be honest, I'm not comfortable in the spotlight. Because of my work in special operations, I have lived most of my adult life in the shadows. It is there that I feel most comfortable. Some people crave attention and accolades. I am not one of them. Now a new chapter in my life is unfolding, and I am much happier! And at the end of the day, isn't that what we are all looking for . . . happiness?

PART I
WAR STORIES

My Life under Fire

I

THE WILL TO WIN

"Surviving a tough situation means staying in the fight and maintaining a warrior's mindset above all else."

—JOSEPH TETI

HAWAII—2013
THE BOAR STORY

MY KILL ZONE WAS arranged on a narrow, high-backed ridge. The warm breeze was constant, rolling in from the shore and bearing southwest, carrying my scent away from the game trail and into the deeper jungle that lay behind me.

There was plenty of fresh boar dung, recent tracks, and every indication that wild pigs regularly used the path in prowling their range. I was surrounded by them. They had overrun that small Hawaiian island. I had seen dozens of the hump-backed, irritable beasts as my partner and I made our way down from the higher elevations, striking out for the shoreline.

We were accompanied by a three-person camera crew that was instructed to keep its distance and remain well hidden when possible. *Dual Survival* was a reality show in the truest sense. The events recorded were authentic and the danger quite real. My partner and I often butted heads over strategy, the mission, and our priorities. But we shared the same goals each time we were thrown together: to survive the situation and to demonstrate the life-saving skills that we suffered much to learn and master.

That day we were playing out a scenario that is all too common: taking on the role of a boar hunter, caught up in the chase, who loses his way in the jungle and takes a fall. As usual, we were tasked by the show's writers to turn around a nearly hopeless situation, save ourselves without assistance, and do it all while filming an entertaining television episode. It's a lot harder than it looks. Trust me on that.

We were provided with an empty butane lighter, mosquito netting, a small game candle, and a hunter's vest. Using just these items, we had to orient ourselves, hike to the coast, and signal rescuers. That day we were functioning as a team. Our chemistry was excellent. By late afternoon we had descended to the island's lower elevations, put together a rough camp, built a fire, crafted a spear for protection, and discovered a source of water that, while not potable, could be boiled and made safe to drink.

The only thing unaddressed was our hunger.

I decided to hunt down and kill a boar for dinner. While I do not enjoy killing animals, in a survival situation I will do what is necessary to replenish the calories and protein that constant exertion and harsh conditions drain from the body. We needed the meat, and I was determined to provide it.

We argued about it. Our differences were stark, which was what gave the show such an entertaining hook. My partner was extremely conservative in his approach to survival. He didn't believe in risks then and doesn't today. His tactics have always been careful, well thought-out, and designed to avoid unnecessary hazards. This strategy worked for him over time. It is a nuanced approach, reflecting years of experience in the Desert Southwest where he also makes his home. Though the conditions are harsh, the American desert is a well-known and more-or-less predictable environment. Reacting in a nonaggressive and risk-adverse manner is a perfect survival approach for that environment.

He often left me frustrated because the *Dual Survival* producers subjected us to exotic terrains and weather conditions that were nothing like New Mexico and Arizona. His approach to survival was much different than mine.

My background as a former Force Recon Marine, US Army Special Forces Green Beret, and as an operative in a top-secret government counterterrorist unit has tested me in dozens of rugged, unforgiving environments and under extreme and violent conditions. Survival in these scenarios requires an aggressive approach at all times and a willingness to take extraordinary, well thought-out, and calculated risks. I do not and will not place myself in harm's way for no reason. I've only got one life. So, the pros and cons must be weighed carefully.

Since survival is my end goal, I study the probabilities before I act— but I act. I will do what is necessary to ensure my safety and to protect those with me. I am never impulsive or rash. But I am unwavering in my convictions. I rely upon my physical abilities, good judgment, and sound tactical strategies that I have utilized to the fullest in the past. They have served me well and saved me many times.

Regarding feral pigs, they are dangerous and highly unpredictable. When aroused or protecting their young, they will attack and have the ability to kill human beings. My partner made the point to me that directly risking injury placed the team in jeopardy. Viewers caught less than a minute of our argument, but in reality, it lasted far longer. Ultimately I decided to pursue the more dangerous course, because I would have done the exact same thing if the cameras weren't rolling. And I wanted to make the point to viewers that one must put aside qualms and do what is necessary in a survival situation. We needed food, and we needed it badly.

I staked out the game trail carefully. I had dismissed several other locations. While they might have worked, they were less than ideal and I leave nothing to chance. I wanted to stack the deck in my favor as much as possible.

I arranged a series of obstacles to steer the targeted animal into an ambush site that I controlled. Here, I placed double-woven snares made from a segment of chicken wire fence I had scavenged from a streambed. In a survival situation, you must recognize the value of raw materials and be prepared to use them in a variety of imaginative ways. Thinking *outside of the box* and building useful tools is critical.

In addition to fashioning snares from the wire, I used it to create a fence to funnel the boar into the trap. I had used this type of tactic before against human enemies in combat. It is a very effective and battle-tested *old-school* linear ambush.

One of the worst-case scenarios I could imagine was the boar escaping my carefully laid trap and charging me. Armed with only a makeshift spear and a knife, I would be nearly helpless. There were no guarantees if my plan went south. There was no question that I risked serious injury and possible death.

I waited for nearly six hours, lying on my belly in the brush, attuned to the environment, to noises, motion, and surrounding odors. I have a keen sense of smell. It was more useful to me than hearing in that situation because wild boars have a powerfully offensive odor. I knew I'd smell the beast coming long before I heard it.

The film crew grew restless. The lead cameraman informed me that they were going to stop filming shortly due to the fading light. I gave him a nod and looked at my watch. With only thirty minutes left there was every reason to believe my carefully crafted plan was about to fall victim to simple darkness.

It was then that an awful stench came rolling down the trail. As anticipated, I smelled the male boar well before he arrived. He was coming down the path, ambling and snuffling as they do, in search of food and popping in and out of sight due to the heavy brush. For a moment he was hidden from my sight by a large rock formation. I thought I'd lost him. But much to my relief, he reappeared immediately. He was a full-grown male, somewhere in the neighborhood of 200 pounds. He was a banquet on the hoof.

The six hours I'd lain in wait had been put to good use. I'd rehearsed every aspect of the kill in my mind. I knew exactly how it would look, sound, and feel. My attack was preplanned, and every countermove of the boar was factored in. I expected the unexpected to occur. I had defined an egress plan and a running path. I had selected trees to climb along that route in case I was wounded, or the boar was simply faster.

I was using a tactic called "crisis rehearsal." It had served me well hundreds of times before as I waited to deploy into hot zones in Afghanistan and Iraq. When the moment of truth arrived, I wanted to react instantaneously and carry out the plan without hesitation.

I kept repeating the tenants of CQB (close quarters battle) to myself: speed, surprise, violence of action. I knew I would be dealing with a deadly animal and a wildly unstable situation.

As the creature approached, I felt adrenaline flooding my system. The chemical reaction of the body to stress can be useful, but this fight or flight instinct is also a potential disruptor to effective action. Distractions are filtered out. Everything goes quiet. Time seems to slow down as the crisis unfolds, giving the individual a narrower range of perceptual responses. But one also develops a sort of mental myopia or "tunnel vision." Your environment and surroundings effectively disappear as you hone in on your target until you can see nothing else.

All of these things happened to me at once. I had experienced this pre-kill aura many times before, but it was strong that day. I was blind to everything except the hulking, feral boar. My breathing grew stronger. My heartrate shot up. My palms were suddenly sweaty. I did my best to control my breathing. I knew that I had prepared fully and the battlefield was in my favor. I have heard it said many times that "luck is where opportunity meets preparation." My opportunity was walking straight into my preparation.

The boar met with the diverting wall I had constructed out of the chicken wire fence, turned aside, and shuffled right into the snares. The world slowed down. I leapt up and moved with lethal intent. As I rushed through the thick brush toward the animal, I was blind to everything except my quarry.

He saw death approaching. His eyes rolled and he panicked, struggling to break the tightly wound wire immobilizing his right rear leg. I was on him in a moment. I aimed for a small area on his body, about the size of a softball and located directly behind his shoulder blades.

With one thrust of the spear I pierced his thick hide and slammed the blade into his heart. Such is the natural resilience and fighting spirit of these creatures that he didn't die from the terrible wound. He only fought harder. I now understand why many of the Roman legions painted stylized boar on their shields. They were honoring the legendary toughness and vigor of the ferocious animals. Such a blow would have dropped a human being on the spot.

In an instant I drew my knife, jumped on the boar's back, and severed his spinal cord. From start to finish the kill took less than ten seconds. I glanced from left to right, as I had been taught, to break the grip of adrenaline on my senses and to regain focus.

In CQB one must recover quickly from a kill because other combatants are likely to present themselves. Some viewers felt this was a visceral reaction to the slaughter, but in actuality it was simply my training kicking in, preparing me for what would come next. Rule number one: Always maintain 360-degree security.

In this case, there were no enemies eager to engage me. There was only a dead boar and a worried partner to contend with. I gutted the pig then and there to lessen its weight. I held its heart and studied it. The spear point had penetrated the heart, inflicting a deep gash that tore through the beating muscle. The wound should have killed the boar immediately. To this day I am impressed with the creature's determination and its will to survive.

I was forced to carry the pig, slinging its carcass across my shoulders. The long hike back with my burden gave me plenty of time to think about how I was going to handle my partner. I felt certain that he would still be in arguing mood.

But he wasn't. He was surprised, impressed, and hungry. My win-at-all-costs mentality resulted in a further cementing of our team and quite possibly the best meal of roast pork I have ever eaten. We survived to fight another day.

We both did what we felt was necessary in order to endure. Survival, like life, is about making correct and informed choices. But it is also about acting when necessary, sometimes with ruthless efficiency.

The fact that you picked this book up says a lot about you. I'm almost sure that you have some familiarity with me and would like to understand what drives an individual to the extremes and into the situations that I have endured. Most likely, something in your past has compelled you to take an interest in survival techniques and you are actively engaged in an effort to broaden your experience and learn more. Perhaps you watched *Dual Survival* and have certain opinions about my methods and ideology. Maybe you are worried about the future, the relative fragility of societal structures, and what may come tomorrow. If any or all of these apply to you, you are a survivor, just like me.

While this book is an autobiography first, it should also be viewed as a survival manual for life that applies to a wide variety of scenarios. In the course of existence, you will encounter situations beyond your control. These are as inevitable as life is random. No amount of planning can eliminate stress, conflict, illness, and finally, death. Nothing can fully prepare you for the trials that will come tomorrow. But a few specific psychological aids will assist you greatly in the struggles ahead, whether you find yourself on a battlefield in the heat of combat, engaged in ritualistic office chores and facing ridiculous deadlines, or worrying about how to pay the bills next month.

Everyone is born. Everyone succeeds and fails. Everyone suffers. Everyone enjoys moments of terror and triumph. Remember that you are not alone. Seven billion people surround you, and they are all struggling for their daily bread and wondering what their next move should be. You are an equal to each and every one of them. But that shouldn't be good enough for you. You should want more. You should endeavor to win at nearly any cost and in every situation. This is only possible if you bring the right tools to bear in the fight. The ability to use preselected survival strategies is crucial. You will learn many approaches here. Some you will develop on your own. These will not only assist you in a crisis, they will also improve your daily life and present you with reasons to keep moving forward. They will give you an advantage that only a few of those many billions possess.

In my personal experience there are six basic tools we all need to develop and hone in order to live well and enjoy what we have. Each of these will be mentioned in coming chapters and expanded upon, but I will state them for you clearly now.

The first tenant is crucial, perhaps as important as all the rest combined. You must have faith. I am a Christian man. I believe in the Lord Jesus Christ as my Savior. Some of you embrace faiths very different from mine and some claim there is no Redeemer. But faith is essential, no matter your belief structure. You must believe in something greater than yourself; perhaps in your wife, the future of your child, the flag, or even, God forbid, in a 600-year-old tree. Whatever you believe, believe in it to the fullest and take comfort in its immediacy. This is crucial to your psychological survival. As a result of my faith, I try to be the best man that I can be every day. Occasionally I stumble and fall short of the mark. I am only human and therefore imperfect. I understand that I am so flawed I cannot begin to comprehend Divine reasoning. No one has ever effectively explained why bad things happen to good people. I take comfort in my faith because it tells me that I will see my lost family and friends again. It gives me a reason to live each day to the fullest.

The second tenant is to have a sense of humor and to understand that life itself is ironic in the best sense of the word. We expect certain things. They rarely happen. Instead, we continually find ourselves in undreamt of circumstances. What would life be without that spice, that variety, and the constant challenge of the unexpected?

The third is an ability to override your basic reactions in the face of stunning upsets and reversals. You must learn to think first and do second. Succumbing to shock and grief will lead to your defeat. *Think* and then act. Far too often people do the opposite. In certain circumstances this can have disastrous consequences.

The fourth is to understand that you are mortal and frail and you cannot control every situation. Learn what you can from failures, sudden successes, and disasters. Study what occurred. Apply your findings. Do not blame yourself for the randomness inherent in daily life.

The fifth is to have a willingness to do what is necessary, not only to survive but to better your environment and the lives of those around you. Helping others succeed was something my father instilled in me at a very young age and something I practice to this very day. We are all selfish in our own ways, but when you stop and turn your selfishness into selflessness, you will find life more peaceful and rewarding.

Sixth is to build a network of supporters and family who you can rely on in lean and dangerous times. While it's certainly possible to go it alone—and I have—I can tell you without hesitation that it's far easier to be part of a large, caring, and responsive team.

I am a survivor. I have survived brutal combat in the worst, most inhospitable regions on the planet. I survived childhood illness, weakness, and the early loss of family. I am part of a growing culture of survivalists and otherwise ordinary men and women who believe in self-improvement. At some point, much to my surprise, I became a television star. The fame was momentary. But for a while, I was part of the superb team that produced *Dual Survival*. Take note of the name. It was not called *Lone Survivor* or *Lone Operator*. The first word in the title of that program was *Dual*. I was part of a team effort, right along with my partner and dozens of supporting staff and millions of fans who encouraged, criticized, and supported us at all times. Without them, we would not have made it to the air. We would not have faced down lions in the African bush, struggled across the blasted wasteland of Chile's Atacama Desert, or spent time together on a desert island, all for the enjoyment and edification of viewers.

If it wasn't for family, one that wasn't even my own, I would not have coped well with the death of my finest friend. I will talk more about him and the lessons his unexpected death taught me in a short while. If it wasn't for my extended TV family, including the legions of loyal fans, there would have been no *Dual Survival*. If it wasn't for you, the individual in search of information who selected this book and effectively became part of my family at the same instant, my story would have remained untold.

If you stay with me through these pages, you will certainly hear more about me, but you will also develop a nuanced and powerful toolbox of survival strategies that will change and greatly enhance the way you live. This is the real purpose of *Lone Operator*. This book is designed to help you help yourself.

You are not alone. You do not have to go it alone. Former lone operator Joseph Teti is in your corner.

2

THE FINAL OPTION

Then I heard the voice of the Lord saying, "Whom shall I send?
And who will go for us?" And I said, "Here am I. Send me!"

—ISAIAH 6:8

BATTLEFIELD AFGHANISTAN
SEVENTY-SEVEN HOURS

"HEY," MARK SAID. "YOU THERE?"

I blinked. For a moment I had been lost in reverie. I was thinking about a different time and a vanished world. I was remembering my childhood in the suburbs of Pittsburgh and the pretend war games I played with my best friend, Bill. Everything, it seemed, from the earliest moments, had led me to that mountainside in Afghanistan. For just a moment I wondered whether I would fulfill my destiny in that place.

I was an operative in one of the most secretive government counterterrorist units in the world. The group was affectionately referred to by our leadership as "America's Attack Dogs."

I was deployed with a handful of other patriots to hunt down those responsible for 9-11. When then-President Bush said, "The gloves are coming off," he was specifically referring to us. No other unit in the US arsenal had the ability or the training to do what we did. Military special operations units are constrained by heavy-handed laws written by politicians who have never experienced combat. We were not. The gloves were indeed off, and those responsible were going to pay and pay big.

I am not permitted to discuss specifics about who I worked for or the missions for ethical, moral and legal reasons. But to put it in perspective, I will say this: The security clearance needed to just serve in this unit was a TOP SECRET SCI. SCI stands for Sensitive Compartmented Information. It is the highest security clearance awarded to an individual. Members of our nation's elite military units like US Army Delta Force and Navy SEAL Team 6 have such clearances. However, the unit I served in also required you to pass an in-depth polygraph test. The identities of operational members of units like Delta and ST 6 are closely guarded secrets while they are serving, but once out, there are no laws or restrictions preventing them from disclosing they were members of those units. The unit I served in requires former operatives to maintain secrecy—for life—of their involvement and association with the unit. I have never, and will never, disclose who I worked for. It was truly as "black ops" as it gets.

"I'm alright," I replied with a certainty I didn't feel. "Let's move out."

It was damn hot. We had departed the chopper a mere ten minutes before, but I was already working up a good sweat.

I was bearded, tan, and in great physical shape. I had trained hard for such scenarios and, to paraphrase the words of the immortal Joan Crawford, "It wasn't my first rodeo." But conditions on the ground are never quite what you expect. You can work up a perfect loadout and an even better plan and you can train until you're confident that every eventuality is covered, but nothing can fully prepare you for the reality of combat. Things go wrong. Murphy is always around the corner. No battle plan can completely account for the unpredictable behavior of human beings, the "Fog of War," or the sheer capriciousness of Mother Nature.

We were wearing light kit, about sixty-five pounds of gear not counting the weapons we had in hand. This included body armor, an assault vest with ammo, and one quart of water total in camelbacks slung over our shoulders. In theory, this outfit was designed for quick movement, not an extended stay in the field. And it was supposed to be light enough so that the summer conditions wouldn't kill us. The result left me feeling like I was roasting slowly over a barbeque pit in hell.

We'd been dropped off two terrain features away from our target, which is an overly complicated way of saying two mountain ranges separated us from the bad guy we were targeting.

He was a midlevel money carrier for the Taliban, what we called a "facilitator." While he wasn't a big fish in any real sense, he had certainly proven troublesome to our efforts to suppress local evildoers and drive the lingering remnants of the Taliban out of our AO (area of operation).

The target was critical to financing insurgents and troublesome warlords and keeping the flow of guns running. Worse yet, he had his hands in all kinds of pies from government corruption to the bribery of local officials. He needed to go away, permanently.

Like any business, an insurgency runs on money. The Taliban was running a Western-style and very businesslike operation that generated basic reports, delivered profits to a few, and provided services to a multitude. But unlike Western businesses, it brutally killed people routinely, including customers who didn't agree with its business plans.

This medium-size fish we were targeting was integral to the web of deceit, bombings, and armed assaults that caused us daily headaches. Taking him out would have changed the local equation significantly.

Fortunately for us, we had learned that he was meeting with three other members of his network, or what we called a "cell." They were gathering for one day in a remote mountain compound. And these extras were much higher up in the food chain.

Unfortunately for us, we had a very narrow window of opportunity in which to strike, about four hours give or take, according to our source. Time was not on our side. The meeting would be brief. The insurgents would share a meal together, then all parties would disperse quickly with the much-needed cash.

Since the meeting was taking place in daylight, we were forced to move in daylight. This is never optimal. Still, the situation demanded an urgent response and we mounted a quick mission that seemed, on the surface, to be just like hundreds of others we had run successfully in the past.

Let it be said that I have always been a good hunter and a better tracker, but I have been the hunter, not the hunted. I didn't anticipate being any such thing that day. I was prepared for every eventuality except that one. As a result of what happened next, I don't hunt anymore. I will not deliberately pick up a rifle and go into the woods to kill a deer. Having been the quarry once, I now understand and empathize. I no longer kill for sport, though I would never discourage anyone who enjoys the hunt from doing so. I encourage it based on the lessons it teaches.

Our mission was simple enough. We were tasked to navigate to high ground above the compound where the bad guys were holed up, to verify the target was there, and then call in an airstrike. At no time were we to approach the buildings or reveal our presence. We were instructed to sit tight through the bombing run, conduct a BDA (battle damage assessment), and then move overland to an extraction point.

As a precaution, Mark and I had carefully mapped out our E&E (escape and evasion) route. These are predesignated routes designed to frustrate pursuing enemies and deliver teams or individuals safely to a pickup point. A lot of planning and backup preparation goes into such a mission. Even failures of intelligence and random chance are factored in. But again, no plan is perfect. Conditions on the ground were such that we knew a planned evacuation might be impossible.

Operators like Mark and I have been described as "the crown jewels in the US special operations community." Such praise is great, but it's usually accompanied by darker, more realistic phrases that apply to a unit like the one I was in. Our place in the grand scheme of things was always made clear to us. Our survival was secondary to national security needs. That's just how it was. There was certainly no gray area about it.

We planned and conducted a broad range of special operations missions covering the entire operational continuum. These missions gave the president of the United States an option when overt military and/or diplomatic actions were not viable or politically feasible.

Operations of this nature require rapid response with surgical application of a wide variety of unique skills while maintaining the lowest possible profile of US involvement. While the Department of Defense would have spared no effort to get us back if captured, however, we were no longer working for the US military. We were members of a superelite government team that was supposed to operate completely below the radar. Though the organization I worked for was committed to my safety without question, and had proven it time and again, I had never felt more alone and exposed than I did that day.

We knew the route. We moved quickly and efficiently in the direction of the compound, confirming our route with a GPS. We encountered no one, not even a stray goat herder. The conditions, it seemed, were perfect for a quick infil and exfil (infiltrate and exfiltrate).

We never made it to the compound. To this day I'm not sure what went wrong or how we were compromised. Perhaps someone saw the helicopter move in and drop us off. There was little foot traffic in the area, and it was remote. But random chance plays a large role in combat. The smallest decision or event can have a devastating impact. No matter the cause, the enemy knew we were present almost from the moment our boots touched the ground.

We walked for a good two hours. The first sign that things had gone sideways was served up in the form of popping, ricocheting rifle fire. Bullets decorated the rocks around us and sent us scurrying for cover.

"What the hell!" I shouted.

I knew immediately that the rounds were coming from small arms, the usual mix of AK-47s and PKMs. The Taliban took full advantage of all of the weapons that the Russians left behind in the '80s, when they departed Afghanistan in a hurry.

Our attackers were well-armed but poorly trained. They had opened fire at quite a distance, at first sight, and insisted on wasting ammunition in a futile effort to mow us down. They didn't even bother to aim because they weren't good at it.

As I hunkered down with Mark behind a patch of boulders, I was already assessing our position. We were lightly armed ourselves, two against a dozen or more bad guys. While they couldn't shoot straight and didn't have much of a plan, they were serious about killing us. They were determined to make that happen. All it would take, I knew, was a lucky bullet or a bad ricochet. You never see the one coming that has your name on it.

We couldn't defend ourselves against a large number of attackers. If we stayed in one place, they would simply outflank us and walk right over our bullet-riddled bodies. Our safest course was to keep moving, gain some distance, backtrack quickly, and call in the helo.

A single wound, even a nonfatal one, would end things quickly for us. Though Arnold Schwarzenegger makes it look easy, you really can't run that well with a bullet in your leg or gut. Knowing Mark, he would have never left me there. He would have gone down fighting right next to me. This is a quality you will always find in special operations teams. It's about the man next to you. Leaving someone in a bad situation is unthinkable.

Fortunately, the scumbags chasing us did not have an RPG (rocket-propelled grenade). If armed with that weapon, poor marksmanship wouldn't have been a stumbling block for them. Just placing a round somewhere nearby is good enough to riddle an enemy with shrapnel or drop him due to blast wounds and concussion injuries. In the conventional sense, it is usually the better course of action to simply overwhelm your enemy, to apply as much firepower as you can from as great a distance as you can, accurately engaging the enemy, without going one-on-one. This minimizes your own casualties and gets the job done.

During the Battle of the Argonne Forest, members of the US 77th Division came under withering fire from German emplacements and retreated to the believed safety of the deep woods, a tangled, wildly overgrown region known as "The Pocket." The Germans knew full well that entering the dense wood and fighting hand-to-hand would result in a bloodbath. So, they shelled the area relentlessly and riddled it with machinegun fire. What killed many of the 77th's soldiers, now known as "The Lost Battalion," wasn't aimed fire or even stray bullets. It was shrapnel and flying splinters from the exploding trees that surrounded them. The Germans understood that winning a battle isn't about marksmanship or honor. It's about killing your enemy, even if you have to use a blunt instrument to do it.

Mark and I didn't waste much time discussing it. He was a realist, and he reached the same conclusions I did just as quickly. He was a twenty-two-year Army veteran and a retired master sergeant. The last twelve years of his career were spent with Delta Force. It would be an understatement to say that he was a highly seasoned operator.

He'd fought in Somalia and responded when the helos went down over Mogadishu. He didn't like talking about what he did or saw that day. I suspect he regretted many things. The experience hardened him. He was tough as old leather and fiercely independent of authority. He was in amazing physical and mental shape and one of the sharpest men I have ever known.

I was lucky to have been with him that day. He was a warrior in the purest sense of the word.

We ran for an hour or two at a time. I cannot stress enough how important it is to be physically fit. Being in "good" shape that day would not have cut it. "Good" wasn't sufficient in that circumstance and never will be in similar dire situations. Discipline and commitment to physical excellence is paramount in special operations. That day it paid off with huge dividends. We were forced to move constantly, rarely pausing, darting from cover to cover, keeping rock outcroppings and dried wadis between us and our pursuers. We had no intention of allowing them to close the time and distance gap. Endurance and physical stamina were crucial in keeping us alive.

After a few tense exchanges with our higher-ups, it became apparent to us that a quick evac was off the table. No one would come to our aid until we managed to shake the fighters on our tail.

Another Blackhawk Down scenario was something feared up and down the chain of command, even within my unit. The realities of who I worked for were made clear on the day I passed from outsider to operative.

"Plausible deniability" was paramount in everything we did. This phrase has been overused by the media and in movies so much that its real meaning is now blurred. Let me clarify. What it means is this: The US government should and absolutely will deny all involvement if one of its clandestine operatives is discovered and/or killed. "Joe who? Never heard of him."

Simple enough. But it has larger implications for those who serve in clandestine units. The real meaning of this policy is that the cavalry will, on occasion, fail to respond and rescue operatives in tough situations. National security interests must be served first. This stark reality was hammered home at every opportunity to me. When we questioned this accepted vulnerability, as everyone does, we were given the option to stay with the program or pack our bags. Some good men departed. I chose to remain.

We kept moving and firing back when our pursuers edged into range. Mark and I were disciplined, firing only when we had clear targets. Due to the particulars of the mission, we were not carrying a normal ammo loadout. Usually we would have been equipped with nine thirty-round magazines for our M4s. But due to the rough terrain and the necessity of speed, we cut our load in half. We carried five mags each, one in the weapon, and four in the vest.

I heard the panicked shouts of wounded men and cries demanding mercy from Allah. We knew our shots were finding their marks. But they kept on coming, angered by our willingness to make the chase difficult. I was surprised by their tenacity. They wanted us dead, or better yet, captured.

They knew we were vulnerable and desperate. They wouldn't have continued the chase over those many miles if they didn't believe the outcome was preordained and inevitable. Like wolves that sense weakness in their prey, they were circling in for the kill. A strange form of claustrophobia was taking over my thoughts, something I have never felt before or since.

When we paused to rest, our relentless, determined hunters closed up the distance one step at a time. They were implacable and tireless. I admired their stamina but not much else about them.

It's okay to detest your enemy, particularly if it keeps you alive a little longer. Being pissed off is a good thing in certain situations. The words of one of my mentors came to mind: "Use controlled rage to your benefit."

Capture was not an option. The Taliban fighters we had met in combat did not practice mercy. I'm not even sure they understood it as a concept. That's how far they had regressed, how completely they had abandoned millennia-old codes of human behavior in pursuit of bloody victory and the perpetuation of their cause.

It's hard for me to believe the movement was more or less spawned by our cooperation with Afghan fighters. At the time we came to their aid, they were resisting the Soviet invasion and occupation of their nation. Evil and ignorant men like Osama bin Laden and Khalid Sheikh Mohammed twisted those who were vulnerable and easily swayed into something unrecognizable from a moral standpoint.

Brutal torture and a slow, lingering death were all I expected from them. They would separate my head from my body when they were done, delighting in my agonized screams. I was sure of my fate then, as sure as I have been at any time. I was going to die, either at their hands or my own. I had no intention of being captured. During my unit training, we were shown videos of the Taliban decapitating individuals. There was no way that was going to happen to me.

Daylight faded, and the chase continued throughout the night. There was no possibility of sleep. We could gain ground on our slower pursuers but only enough to pause and catch our breaths. Then they were on us again. Rounds popped and whined all around our position and spurred us to keep moving.

As dawn approached, we abandoned the Level-IV ceramic plates we wore under our assault vests. The weight was slowing us down, and wearing them made us sweat profusely. We agreed the armor wasn't going to save us anyway. The enemy was conducting textbook recon by fire, showering us with rounds to force us into the open. Speed and movement were our only advantages.

In our case, speed was security. The faster we could depart the area, the better our odds were of escaping in one piece. The front and back plates weighed sixteen pounds. With that weight gone, we were refreshed, more comfortable, and maneuverable. Still, the fix was only temporary. We were slowing down, and we knew it.

At that point we were suffering badly from exhaustion and the onset of dehydration. We had gone through our water supplies and consumed the few Power Bars we'd tucked into our vests during the hurried departure. There was nothing to eat or drink in that desolate corner of the Afghan wilderness. There was nothing at all. The streambeds were dry. Game had gone elsewhere in search of water. Only rocks and the miserable fundamentalist fighters and their American quarry remained.

Now Mark and I were the hunted. It was a strange and terrible feeling to know that a powerful, motivated enemy was pursuing us and there was almost nothing we could do to change the situation.

With determination, we could stave off the end for a little while. But it was coming, and we had more or less made our peace with it.

Mark was quick with a joke or to make fun of me. He had a habit of softening any difficult situation with piercing wit. That was normal Mark. Toward the evening of the second day he had acquired a haunted look that I didn't like.

As evening fell we were beginning to accept that there would be no third night. We were in poor shape, the conditions were deteriorating, and we were running out of ammo. But as bad it was, Mark kept me laughing.

We carried E&E maps with us, upon which we'd clearly marked our egress route. These proved worthless. We were forced off the path by our hunters and crossed and recrossed the same ground numerous times. Our tracks must have looked like a wild zigzagging nightmare.

In a moment that stands out in my mind, Mark pulled his E&E map from his cargo pocket, gazed at it with disdain, then tore off an entire quarter of the map. When I asked him why he did that, he explained that it was more useful as toilet paper.

We kept up a good pace and moved steadily westward, hoping to draw the fighters far from their base and resupply points and into the harder, hotter terrain of the foothills. We hoped they'd grow frustrated and simply go home.

Somehow, we survived the second night and lived to see the dawn of what we thought could be our last day on Earth. Mark pulled me to a halt and asked how many rounds of ammo I had. I told him I had one magazine left.

He became insistent. He wanted to know exactly how many rounds I was carrying. It wasn't an unusual request. Checking one's ammo count is a good way to gauge life expectancy in a gun fight, particularly when the crap is hitting the fan in a big way.

I told him I had one in the chamber and seven in the mag.

He said, "I'd put one of those rounds in your pocket."

I wondered why he would suggest such a thing. His rationale for the odd request only became clear to me in hindsight. He was telling me to save a round for myself. He was telling me that he didn't think we were going to make it out of there. And he didn't think being captured was an acceptable alternative to suicide.

On reflection, I don't know that I could have killed myself. I'm a survivor. I will do anything to go on. I like to think I have courage. But I can't imagine putting a bullet in my head, even in such a high-stakes situation. I would have hesitated despite the inevitability of brutal torture and a slow, grueling death at the hands of a merciless enemy. I know this about myself. If Mark was dead and I was left with only a bullet, I would have used it against them and not myself. It's simply the way I'm built.

I thought of my wife back home, wishing I had bought more insurance when I had the chance. I remembered the childhood war games I'd played with my best friend, Bill. As a boy I had a sense of inevitability, of destiny. I knew I was going to do something special with my life. It didn't seem right to me that my story was about to end on a rocky hillside in the middle of Afghanistan. The irony of the situation was almost funny.

I placed the round in my pocket as instructed.

I never had to make that decision. As it turned out, one of our pilots took his life in his hands and came after us. I'm not sure whether he was motivated by the desperate calls we made to our base or if there was a sudden change of heart on the part of our unit's leaders. I never learned the truth. Perhaps it was a combination of both.

I tend to believe the man exercised his initiative, defied authority, and came to our rescue despite the declared consequences. It made sense. Cliff was a former Task Force 160 pilot, a unit that produced some of the best and most daring helicopter pilots in the world. I seriously doubt such an individual would have been able to live with himself knowing that men died while he sat by idly.

I heard the steady thump of the blades long before the chopper arrived. It was a beautiful sound.

The fighters came for us at a dead run. They knew our rescuers were on the way. Worse, we were backed up against the cliff of a deep wadi. The bank of the ancient riverbed was steep, and the fall would certainly have injured if not killed us outright. There was simply nowhere else to go, and the helo could not have arrived at a more fortuitous moment.

Cliff had no intention of putting the bird down. He was flying a monstrous Soviet-built MI-17. This helo is equipped with a stern ramp, and the steel platform was already open and locked when he swung the craft into position. He dropped the aircraft below the lip of the wadi and positioned the ramp so it was a mere three or four feet from our position. The massive rotors were dangerously close. The wash from the whirling blades nearly knocked me over. We abandoned all caution in our eagerness to get aboard.

Mark went first, leaping the gap with an enviable athlete's grace. I heard shots and impacts as close as a foot away. I felt the time had come to make my own move. I thought of hungry sharks and floating sailors from the USS *Indianapolis* tragedy, which was very odd. I felt a similar urgency to get the hell out of the water. I leapt.

A precious second passed, during which I was fully airborne and my ears were filled with the angry chatter of machinegun fire. Somehow, the insurgents had gotten hold of heavier weapons. As I jumped, the helo caught a downdraft and rolled to port. I struck the ramp face-first. The bird rolled again as it lifted off. I slid all the way to the starboard bulkhead on my stomach. I was deeply jealous of Mark's Hail Mary leap and perfect form.

He was squatting near me and clapped my shoulder with brotherly affection. He shouted over the noise of the rotors and wind, "There. That wasn't so bad, was it?"

Later at our debrief we found out that we'd endured seventy-seven hours of straight pursuit and covered eighteen miles of mountainous terrain. We were suffering from exposure, and we'd each lost somewhere in the neighborhood of ten pounds. "No," I agreed. "That was fucking awesome!"

To this day I keep the bullet that Mark told me to save for myself. It sits on a shelf in my house, a silent reminder that nothing in this world is guaranteed or predictable. The bullet is a visual reminder that making my mind and body tough is the best survival strategy I ever implemented. Just seeing it makes me want to head to the gym or go for a run. It also says to me without question that I have the necessary courage to do what is required, even in the most unforgiving circumstances. Finally, it reminds me that my destiny wasn't fulfilled on a mountainside in Afghanistan. Something greater still awaits.

One particular topic comes up repeatedly in interviews and in random encounters with those I meet. Inevitably, no matter the subject or how the conversation began, the discussion always gets around to fear. People want to know more about fear and how to deal with it effectively. I am usually asked to describe the most terrifying moment in my life.

I can say without a doubt that I was most shaken in the quiet moment when Mark told me to put a round in my pocket. There was no shooting, no yelling, and no screaming. I heard only a gentle suggestion from a friend. A day earlier I would have disagreed that such a little thing could frighten me so badly. But days pass, and life's unpredictability can change everything in a heartbeat.

Life is an interior struggle similar to an external battle. In battle, there are rules. We call these the rules of engagement. Such directives lay the groundwork for how we fight. In a similar manner, we should draw up rules to define how we live. I will be giving my rules as we proceed. I don't expect my personal choices to work for everyone. Your life is yours alone, and the rules will be unique to you. As long as you take a few things from this narrative and apply them to yourself, you will undoubtedly gain and prosper.

3

THE WARRIOR MINDSET

"You can live three weeks without food, three days without water, and three minutes without air, but you won't last three seconds without the will to survive."

—JOSEPH TETI

BATTLEFIELD IRAQ
I'M HIT!

BY THE SUMMER OF 2008, the fight in Iraq had gone on without pause for five straight years. Saddam was dead. Most of his cohorts had been captured or killed. The Republican Guard was completely out of business, and all the tacky gold-plated vestiges of the Hussein regime had been pulled down.

A civilian politician and businessman named Nouri al-Maliki replaced the dictator as civilian leader following the first legitimate democratic vote held in that country in nearly fifty years. If you think all that sounds great and peace should have ensued, I can see where you're coming from. You can be forgiven for thinking the end of an armed conflict always leads to love and harmony. But you'd be dead wrong in this case, as well as most others. Peace and kumbaya do not happen naturally. They have to be worked at, and folks need to want an end to conflict. It was obvious to me that the Iraqis were still in a combative mood.

Following the vote, al-Maliki, who seemed like a bright fellow, got straight to work pissing off the Sunni minority and pretty much everybody who supported him, including dear old Uncle Sam. You might remember that he cozied up to the Iranians and called his American saviors "invaders." His policies caused a full-fledged rebellion, and sectarian violence took root in the towns and cities. It seemed that the folks in Iraq liked killing each other and were prepared to do so at the drop of a hat.

ISIL, later ISIS, was born in the midst of that chaos, declared itself a worldwide caliphate, and went on to wreak havoc. So much for kumbaya. The US military presence in Iraq got larger, and the job of maintaining peace grew more complicated.

My unit was overworked. We were tasked with numerous missions of national importance ranging from erasing high-value terrorists to cleaning up local criminals. We were busy all the time. We were operating at a high level and improving consistently, which was bad news for the evildoers. Tasks that would have challenged us a year before now seemed mundane. I was riding high and feeling bulletproof, which is never a good place to be.

In June of that year we were conducting raids on northern targets, very close to the Turkish border. We were ordered to capture an arms dealer who was making life difficult for everyone.

The dealer had sequestered himself in a remote compound and arranged for a very large money transfer. Cash is the lifeblood of the arms business. Without continuous infusions of hard currency, the bullets don't fly because no one can move or sell the rifles necessary to fire them.

Our target was ridiculously greedy. Still, he had above-average intelligence and impressive escape skills. He didn't linger long at any one location, and he switched the SIM cards in his phones routinely. He employed a terrific network of spies who watched our movements and alerted him the minute we departed our base. He had slipped the noose so many times that we thought of him in legendary terms. He was a real Houdini who played for keeps, not fame.

Our primary source, who had proven himself consistently reliable over time, provided us with a crucial piece of information. He handed over Houdini's schedule. This included locations and dates and times when he would be vulnerable. Based on that data, we calculated that he would be in the compound for a mere three hours. The info was good for a one-time-only use. We had to make it count. Houdini was what we called a TST, a time-sensitive target.

He'd chosen his meeting place carefully. It was heavily fortified, walled off, and protected by a heavy steel door. His window of exposure was a narrow one. Worse, the meeting and money transfer were taking place in broad daylight. The approaches to the complex were fully exposed. There was no sneaking up on our quarry. We were going to have to go in hard and heavy. I often wished the bad guys would make it easy for us, but they almost never did.

Since stealth wasn't an option, we used the only advantages available to us, speed and surprise. We came up the hill like bats out of hell, riding heavily armored Toyota Hilux trucks. We roared to a stop in front of the compound in a haze of dust. The entry team rolled out and planted a breaching charge on the big steel door within ten seconds. It went like clockwork, until it all fell apart.

That day I was providing security for a working dog team tasked with scouting the perimeter wall. We were attempting to locate and seal any escape routes. I was accompanied by an Iraqi commando named Ibrahim, a good man with more nerve than a bum tooth.

The breaching charge went off and alerted a bunch of bad guys holed up in a neighboring compound, a gang of idiots with AK-

47s and assorted small arms. Somehow, we had missed them in our initial survey. They were just itching to get into a disastrously one-sided firefight with a bunch of well-armed, kill-happy Americans. I can say we obliged them, but not for several chaotic moments.

My Iraqi friend and I were the first recipients of a lot of wild and indiscriminate gunfire. The goons sprayed us with dozens of rounds. They missed of course. Your average Iraqi insurgent isn't well-trained or battle-hardened and hasn't practiced with actual firearms. They tend to get excited by the bang-bang noises. They forget to aim, and they pop off lots of rounds in the hope of accidentally hitting something. They do hit lots of things, but it's pretty rare for them to actually nail an intended target. I didn't feel particularly endangered that day, though there was a lot of lead in the air.

We retreated along with the dog and took cover behind the trucks. I heard lots of spangs and pings as rounds bounced off the steel-plated vehicles. I heard our teams communicating as they systematically cleared the compound.

I felt the bad guys should have been aiming, or working on outflanking us, or anything that was tactically beneficial to their side. But they continued to waste ammo and yell hoarsely.

Now and then, Ibrahim would pop up his head to scout the shooters and radio positions and angles to the fire team that was already moving against them. Things were going well. The bad guys were in real trouble. They had bitten off far more than they could chew. They seemed ignorant about the true nature of their American enemy. Units like the one I was in are disciplined and deadly. Better yet, they take the time to aim and don't send rounds downrange unless they're sure of hitting their intended target. Wasting ammo is a sin in our line of work. The idiots next door were just about to meet Allah.

I moved to the end of the vehicle to survey a section of the street that Ibrahim couldn't see. As I neared the rear bumper, I felt a stinging blow to my shin. I was staggered but managed to keep my balance. I looked down and saw a small round hole in my uniform pants. There was very little blood, and the injury didn't feel serious. Still, it burned like hell. I understood then that I'd been hit.

I had never been shot. I had assumed all sorts of things would happen when I eventually caught a round, that there would be a lot of yelling and blood pouring out of me and people swarming all over my prone body with needles and tourniquets. None of that occurred. I was wounded, but no one appeared to notice. Ibrahim was talking up the radio while the other members of my unit were busily moving against the bad guys. Even the dog didn't pay me any mind. I was a little flustered by the lack of attention. Then I got mad at the hooting idiots on the wall. I knew that was the proper place to direct my rage. For a moment I considered going over there and kicking their asses all by my lonesome. I might have done it too. But I had to know just how badly I was hurt.

I knelt and rolled up my pants leg. I observed that the injury was minor and couldn't have been caused by a bullet impacting my shin. For a moment I was mystified. Then I understood that I had caught a fragment, probably from a round that ricocheted off the truck bottom. I was relieved. Don't get me wrong, knowing you just absorbed a round, fragment or not, is an eye-opener. The reality of my situation struck me at once. All the choices I'd made leading to taking a bullet crystallized in my mind. I was playing on a two-way live-fire range, and up to that moment, the bad guys had always gotten the worst of it.

I rolled down my pants leg and got back to work.

As fast as the shooting started, it was over. The goons on the wall had been wasting ammo indiscriminately for a while. They had probably expended hundreds of precious rounds in the opening minutes of the firefight. Doubtless, what was in their magazines was all they carried, so reloading wasn't an option. They stopped shouting "Allahu Akbar" and fell silent. Ibrahim reported that they disappeared from sight. The shooting was over, and the compound was secured. When my team made it to the roof, they found lots of shell casings, some half-eaten shawarma sandwiches, and not much else. I presume Allah's boys hotfooted it for the hills. It was really the only sensible thing they did that day.

Like many of the missions we conducted, this one was a dry hole, meaning the arms dealer we were sent to collect wasn't home. Houdini had escaped our clutches again. Either our intelligence was flawed, or the man had been tipped off that we were approaching in a hurry.

My anger evaporated. I took a few deep breaths. I still had a job to perform. I had a responsibility to report my injury. I might have ignored the little wound. I was embarrassed at drawing attention to something so small. I had seen men sustain terrible injuries in combat. In comparison, catching a tiny piece of shrapnel seemed laughable.

Craig, our team leader or TL, had positioned himself in a vehicle flanking ours. He'd chosen not to enter the breached building. When we began taking fire, he remained outside on the radio, prepared to call in help if we needed it. I had a lot of respect for Craig, and I appreciated that he always did the right thing, like covering our six that day. Still, he had a weird sense of humor.

I walked over and reported that I had taken a small piece of a round to my right shin.

Immediately he responded, "Didn't your mom tell you not to play with guns?"

I didn't know what to say at first. He kept a straight face, and I wasn't sure he was joking. As I indicated, his sense of humor was a little awkward and off-putting. Finally, I understood that he was trying to put me at ease. I laughed. I did feel better, mentally at least. The wound throbbed like a wasp sting and had an unusual burning sensation.

Craig asked me if I was okay. I told him I was and asked to be examined by a medic just in case. I was an 18B or Special Forces weapons sergeant, not a "qualified" medic. Like everyone in my unit, I had plenty of cross-training in combat trauma procedures, and I had seen a lot. I could patch bullet holes and administer IVs. I was fully capable of keeping a gunshot victim alive for a while until he could be placed in the hands of a qualified medic or a medical professional. I certainly could have "doctored" myself, but that's rarely a smart idea. It's a last-ditch option to be saved for a time when you're alone and you know help isn't coming.

When you are working with the finest medics in the business, every one of them equivalent to, and five times as experienced, as an average paramedic, why break out the Band-Aids on your own?

Our medics were minimally 18D qualified. I won't go into what that means because it's unnecessary for the purposes of the story. Just understand that these guys are an impressive bunch, many of them fully trained as EMTs and paramedics. The series of qualifications they had to pass to work in units like this was grueling, the most difficult in the military by far. I trusted them completely.

Craig called over one of our medics. I knew him as Alan. He inquired about the particulars of the injury. I told him what I surmised, that I had been struck by shrapnel from a ricocheting round and it didn't seem too bad. He was concerned about my pain level. I told him the wound had a powerful sting and burn at first, but right then the pain was easing. The bleeding had stopped on its own. He cleaned up the wound and patched it with a bandage. He informed me that it was a temporary fix. He wanted to examine me further when we reached our forward operating base. We needed to move. It's never smart to hang around an objective once the door has been kicked in. Word travels fast and armed retaliation from a bunch of pissed-off locals is likely.

I was surprised that I'd been shot. For a time, I didn't believe such a thing was possible. I had been walking around with a completely unearned "I'm bulletproof" complex. That's how Custer got his. That's how I got mine. Mind you, the enemy, the situation, and the end results were wildly different, but the root cause was the same. We had walked in the fire and emerged safely every time. We had begun to believe the enemy couldn't touch us. They *can* touch you.

They *will* touch you. If you play at this game long enough, you'll suck up a round. It doesn't matter how good you are. It's inevitable. There were plenty of World War II combat veterans who walked clear across Europe under fire, surviving it all, only to meet brutal ends on a beach in Normandy, France.

The point of this story is that you must maintain a warrior mindset. That mindset does not allow for vanity, delusions of omnipotence, or behaving stupidly in the face of incoming fire. I made no mistakes that day. I maintained situational awareness. I took cover as necessary. I picked up the slack when I realized my buddy Ibrahim did not have a good view of the battlefield. I did my job and stayed focused. Nonetheless, a freak event, a spray of metal fragments from a ricocheting bullet, nearly took me down.

I could have thrown in the towel at that moment. But I didn't. I kept a warrior's mindset and did my job. I was fully prepared in the event that the situation turned and we began taking hits. I didn't lose my temper. Though I wanted to, I didn't charge into the neighboring compound hell-bent on revenge. I took care of myself first, with my thoughts always on my team. I stayed frosty right back to the base.

Plenty of otherwise courageous people go to pieces at the sight of their own blood. Worse, they engage in depressed circular thinking, in endless rounds of "why me" questions that naturally lead to reflections on the unfairness of life, which tug their minds right back to the "why me" question. This self-licking ice cream cone of a feedback loop is completely self-destructive. It isn't consistent with the warrior mindset. The universe isn't going to offer you answers or salvation. But the warrior mindset will save you.

Dozens of books have been written on the subject of the *warrior mindset*. I've agreed with some of what I've read. But it became clear to me after a little study that the majority of the authors putting pen to paper had never experienced a real-world crisis or lingered long on a battlefield. Their perspectives on the matter were technically correct, but they couldn't get at the heart of the matter. They couldn't do so because they hadn't experienced an emergency that required a direct application of this fearsome mindset.

I have used the warrior mindset to my advantage throughout my career. I utilized it in combat. I'm still here to talk about my experiences. I brought it to the table as a tool while filming *Dual Survival.* I am still alive and still sane.

In my never-to-be-humble opinion, the warrior mindset is what separates the men from the boys when crap is really hitting the fan in a big way. The most respected and feared warrior cultures in history cultivated the mindset in their children. Those children grew up to be Spartan hoplites and Samurai warriors.

A "combat" mindset is possessed by those who are able to screen out distractions, push aside stress, and focus on the mission at hand. Ernest Hemingway, one of my favorite authors, picked precisely the right words to describe it: "grace under pressure."

On December 7, 1941, Raymond Haerry was a twenty-year-old Navy coxswain. He was stationed aboard the USS *Arizona.* He'd spent an uneventful morning ferrying fellow crewmembers to and from Ford Island on a motor whaleboat. He didn't think anything of it when he heard the drone of a sizable number of aircraft approaching battleship row. He was having a smoke and didn't sense that anything was amiss.

Moments later Ray heard the popping of rounds striking *Arizona's* teak deck. He recognized that the incoming aircraft were strafing his ship, and they weren't American. He ran like hell for his battle station, a midship antiaircraft battery. Once there, he found that the ammo for the gun was locked up tight. He recognized that the planes were coming in low over the water, too low for the AA guns to be effective. He gathered up his team, and they weighed whether to pry open an ammo box and break the gun loose from its moorings.

The plan might have worked. But just then an armor-piercing bomb went through the deck near turret two and detonated in the forward powder magazine. The resulting explosion lifted *Arizona* right out of the water and broke her back. A fireball raced through the ship killing more than a thousand crewmen in an instant.

Ray was blown right off the deck and into the harbor. He swam to Ford Island, which was seventy yards from the crippled, burning *Arizona*. He encountered body parts and the charred remains of his shipmates. Eventually, he made it ashore and went straight to a machinegun emplacement. He manned the gun throughout the attack and all afternoon. Then, when it became clear that the Japanese had gone, he returned to the harbor and helped pull bodies from the water.

Raymond Haerry displayed grace under pressure. He was and is the epitome of a soldier experiencing severe duress who exhibited the warrior mindset. He remained alert and in the fight. He battled his way through the worst military disaster that had ever been visited upon the United States. At no point did he surrender the will to fight, not when he found his gun useless, when he found himself in the harbor, or even when the battle was done. He could have walked to an infirmary to have his wounds treated. He could have given up the fight and allowed others to handle things. After all, he was injured. He was traumatized. No one would have blamed Ray for throwing in the towel. But he fought on because the lives of others were at stake. When the battle was done, he collected the bodies of his fallen comrades because their families were going to need closure. Just let that sink in.

Without a doubt, the warrior mindset is one of the most overlooked, least discussed aspects of combat and survival training. Having this mindset is critical to one's survival in a life-threatening crisis. In my opinion, it is a pity that all American soldiers aren't taught the value of the *mindset* or given the keys to this crucial tool.

I've provided you with examples of the warrior mindset. Now you deserve a clear definition of the term. It's fairly simple to understand. You must think and act as a true warrior does. You must adopt the mentality of a highly disciplined, focused soldier who fights *not* for himself or personal objectives, but *always* for the sake of others. From the legionnaires of ancient Rome to modern American fighting men, this principle has held true. Over and above the greater cause, we fight for others. When the bullets are flying, we fight for the man or woman standing beside us, not for some flag or ideology. When the combined Germanic tribes under Arminius swarmed three Roman legions in the Teutoburg Forest, those tough, veteran warriors in heavy bronze armor weren't thinking of Rome. They were thinking of one another and looking for a way out.

To cultivate the warrior mindset, you must apply **three core principles**:

1. **Move only when it benefits your cause.**
2. **Harness your inner beast.**
3. **Remain in the fight, no matter the odds.**

It doesn't matter whether you are on a battlefield, caught in a survival situation, engaged in a cutthroat business deal, or trying to raise a pack of children. Apply these three principles and your chances of success will increase significantly. Like the few survivors of the Varian Disaster, you will live to see Rome again and fight another day. Like Raymond Haerry, you will battle on, no matter the cost, to ultimate victory. Like me, you will turn a wound into a reason to fight.

Regarding the first principle, *move only when it is beneficial to your cause*, I mean this: Know yourself, know your motivations, and have a clear-cut set of goals in place. Do these things before making any aggressive changes in your life or battle plan. Charging into a fortified compound all by myself would not have served the mission or assisted my team in the fight. It would have gotten me killed. Instead, I turned my outrage on its head, remained in place, and did my job. Raymond Haerry stuck to his guns all day. The Romans fought back-to-back despite overwhelming odds. Not one of them made a break for freedom and safety. The few survivors of that terrible day owed their lives to the valiant men who remained in place. In Sun Tzu's masterpiece *The Art of War*, he said, "A kingdom that has once been destroyed can never come again into being; nor can the dead be brought back to life." He couldn't have been more right.

As to the second principle, *let loose the beast inside you*, here's what I mean: Commit to the struggle fully and without hesitation. Do what needs to be done to save the day, your fellow soldiers, or the deal. Fight like hell until no one else is left standing on the field. Use any tool at your disposal to quell the enemy, whether it's a broadsword or an Excel spreadsheet. And never be ashamed of your passion and commitment to the cause. Passion is extremely contagious. And if your life is on the line, give no quarter to the enemy. You must be devoid of feeling for their well-being, as they most certainly will not have any for you.

Finally, we will discuss the third and most important principle: *Never surrender the will to fight.* This one is the simplest to understand but the hardest to put into action. We're designed with a fight or flight instinct. Physical preservation is wired into our DNA. When the battle seems overwhelming, we're supposed to run away. Staying put and fighting on is antithetical to our species. But we're more than our DNA. Each of us has the ability to ignore pain, fight for a higher cause, and persevere to victory. The first caveman to pick up a rock and drive off a hungry predator changed our way of thinking. Since we didn't have the physical tools to protect ourselves, like claws and fangs, we were forced to use brains and cunning to endure. We've gotten a lot better at survival since then. Our mental horizons have expanded significantly. We understand that the survival of our species rests not on selfishness and individual gain, but on combining our efforts in a greater cause. The old adage about the weakest link in a chain is true. If you don't surrender the will to fight, the man next to you will struggle on, and the man next to him will do the same. Never surrender. There's too much riding on your shoulders.

Regardless of the training you have received, the gear you may have at your disposal, or the tactics you apply in a given situation, **nothing matters** if you don't have the mindset to persevere. It's just that simple. Even if your technical skills and equipment are flawed, maintaining a "fighting" mindset, the warrior mindset, will save the day.

I've observed this personally during extended deployments to Afghanistan and Iraq. This point was really driven home for me while observing Afghan commandos in blistering firefights. These guys were trained well and had good gear, but what always impressed me was their positive attitude and ability to tap into the warrior mindset when needed. They could turn it off like a switch too. When the rifle fire died, these determined, fearless warriors tucked that mindset away and became happy guys who liked to crack jokes, dream big, and make fun of life in general.

Mark my words: The warrior mindset is the most formidable and useful tool you will take into combat or life. It is a learned skill. It needs to be studied and understood before it can be deployed to maximum potential. Special operations units like the one I served with in Afghanistan and Iraq understood better than anyone the importance of this fearsome psychological asset. We all have the ability to develop a warrior mindset. Gender, age, or what you do for a living aren't factors. I can tell you without hesitation that my ability to tap into the mindset has not only saved my life numerous times but has propelled my personal and business life further than any other life skill.

4

PLANNING FOR THE WORST

"The supreme irony of life is that hardly anyone
gets out of it alive."

—ROBERT HEINLEIN

SIERRA PELONA FOOTHILLS—FEBRUARY 2013
THE HELO CRASH

IN MY LINE OF work, death comes with the territory. It's
something you learn to accept. People around you are going to die,
and sometimes no amount of training, preparation, or situational
awareness is going to prevent it.

It isn't a pleasant thought, and I sometimes have difficulty with
it, but I made my peace long ago on battlefields in Afghanistan and
Iraq and as far back as my childhood when I lost my mother at a
young age.

Still, when death finds your best friend, thousands of miles from the bullets and mortar fire, it's amazing how quickly the walls you have worked so hard to build can crack.

Looking back now, I know I was in shock from the moment I heard those terrible words.

The helicopter crashed.

I simply reacted. As most individuals with military or law enforcement experience do in a crisis of mounting proportions, I instinctively reverted to my training.

We were filming that day, working on a pilot for a survival skills series ordered by the Discovery Channel. The show involved testing a crew of veteran Special Forces operatives in a variety of dangerous scenarios. I had departed the military years earlier for a career as an operator with a little-known government counterterrorism unit. It was a pleasure to be back in the company of old friends, doing what I had always enjoyed most.

I think they're all dead.

The young intern who relayed the information to me was pale and running on auto. She was afraid and visibly shaken to the point of turmoil.

I didn't reply, argue, or demand details. I left my cup of hot coffee and the warmth of the Winnebago that served as our production office. I got into a jeep and headed straight for the crash site.

I knew it was bad, but I wasn't ready to accept it just then. I thought I could make it right. I find problems, and I fix them. That's what I do. I had it in my mind that if I showed up with enough muscle and stubbornness, I could fix this too. I could save my best friend.

My last words to him had been unhappily brusque. He was kneeling by the helicopter in the dark, checking a rucksack. "Mike," I said to him, "it's cold as hell up there. I hope you dressed warm."

That was it. I wished I had said something with feeling. I stepped on the gas. I had to get there ASAP, now, sooner than that, yesterday. I was running on adrenaline. In another scenario, it might have cost me my life.

In moments of sheer terror our higher functions desert us. We go to what we know. The special operations community is acutely aware of the "psychological deficit" brought on by incredible stress. That's why they don't waste time teaching mundane tasks—at least not at first. The numbingly routine chores come later. The first thing they hammer home is that you must get up, move forward, and directly confront hostile forces threatening your safety. We do what most would not—run toward the danger, not away from it. And that's exactly what I did.

Any military special operations personnel or government operative is forged like a razor-sharp knife with one purpose: to find the problem and fix it. We will do nearly anything to "fix the problem," whether it means kicking in a door to the bad guy's house knowing full well that there is going to be a gun fight, exiting an aircraft at 25,000 feet in the middle of the night with eighty pounds of kit on in search of a drop zone fifteen miles away the size of a football field, or killing an armed assailant with a knife because we're out of bullets. The key element here isn't the method of dealing with the problem. It's confronting the source, going to it not away from it, and bringing hell with you. This is the warrior mindset in its purest form.

It was 0330. The temperature had dropped into the low twenties. I cannot remember a blacker night in my life. There is a sort of primal darkness that blankets the Sierra Pelona foothills in California that doesn't exist anywhere else. It's one of the most primitive places on Earth, and it has remained virtually unchanged since our earliest ancestors struggled over those jagged ridges, armed with bone tools, desperately hungry and in search of game.

Out in the California foothills, there is no life. The glow of electric illumination and bright cityscapes are conspicuously absent. The brutal slopes of the rugged uplands are mostly denuded of trees and scrubs. The whole country, high and low, is stripped bare and exposed to the sky. The blazing star fields are always visible and cast a pale radiance over everything.

It is a hopeless, lonely place, and I felt that loneliness deeply as I raced through the darkness, determined to help my friend.

I'd known Mike for more than twenty years, and we'd been tight from the moment we met. If you're lucky in life, you get to call one guy like Mike Donatelli your best friend. Dozens of people I know claimed Mike as their best friend. He was like that. People admired and loved him without reservation. He had a spine of steel wrapped with uncompromising sense, integrity, and endless faith in his Creator. He walked the walk. He did very little talking that was unnecessary. He lived when he should have died again and again. I found it impossible to believe that he was gone. He should have been there to lighten the mood. He was naturally gifted at making someone laugh, even when laughing was the last thing they had in mind.

I couldn't shake the feeling that the intern had given me. The drive must have taken minutes, but it seemed like hours. I couldn't wrap my mind around her words.

The helicopter crashed.

The helicopter had been ordered up to perform a late-afternoon and night-filming run. The pilot, David Gibbs, was a former military veteran himself who took safety damn seriously.

He had lined up every member of the production crew in front of the helo earlier that day and given us a lecture on the do's and don'ts. I remember there were a lot more don'ts than do's. I had flown as a passenger aboard numerous types of helos over my career. I had the routine down cold. But I respected his commitment, and I knew many of the young staff members had never encountered a powerful beast like a Bell 206 Jet Ranger. The education was important, whether they were scheduled to fly or not.

I reached the crest of the hill, which should have given me an expansive view of the crash site. There was no activity. It was quiet as a tomb. First responders are often surprised by the complete silence and stillness that attends a disaster scene. But I'm not. People don't move or speak when they're dead. The lack of noise and movement told me everything I needed to know.

I saw nothing at first. The darkness was thick and nearly impenetrable. Then I spotted a single flashlight beam. It was moving wildly. I was separated from it by nearly a mile. I was sure it was Mike; if anyone was going to walk away from a downed aircraft intact, it was Mike Donatelli. It would be just like him to ignore his injuries, find a light in the wreckage, and go to work. Tending to the wounded would be his first priority, over and above his own safety.

I took off at a dead run, stumbling over spiky brush and sharp stones. I descended into a steep valley, an ancient lakebed that had been dry for a million years or more.

Mike's okay, I thought as I reached the edge of the crash site. I knew I'd hear his booming voice calling out to me, "What took you so damn long, partner? I got a busted knee here, and you're late with the Band-Aids."

But it was Dale Comstock, not Mike, who I encountered. Though I was nominally in charge, I had hired Dale and Mike as equal partners. We shared the necessary tasks and assignments required in planning and filming the show. We decided things amicably, usually talking them over while leaning against the steel Winnebago that served as the centerpiece, canteen, and bunkhouse of our little operation.

The three of us were veterans of multiple service branches and elite Special Forces units. We had been through the fire together and emerged stronger. We were experienced, knowledgeable and certain that we were in control. Putting together a survival show for the Discovery Channel was a new test, but the challenges were relatively minor in scope. After multiple tours for each of us in Afghanistan and Iraq, mastering camera angles and dreaming up trials of outdoor skill seemed to us like small potatoes.

The flashlight beam was weak. It provided just enough illumination so that I could see Dale's ashen face. His eyes were wide and stunned. In a voice I will never forget, he said, "They're all gone, Joe. They're all dead."

"Where's Mike?" I asked. It was sinking in. This was not Dale's first brush with death. He was a veteran of numerous hard-fought conflicts. He had lost many friends. He had taken lives himself as required. But his face told me all I needed to know. I understood at once that something enormous had happened. One of my dearest friends was really gone.

"Where is he?" I demanded.

Dale pointed. "Forty yards that way. Don't go over there." His last words still haunt me. I took the light from him and went. I'm trained to do that. I find problems, and I fix them.

I was still running on autopilot. I was following years of training without realizing it. I remember a story about a young DEA agent who was involved in a drug bust that went south. There was a ferocious firefight, and the veteran detectives with him died almost immediately. The young agent, terrified beyond comprehension, did what he had been taught to do. His first days of instruction at the academy had included hours of qualifications at the firing range. When they found his body, his pockets were filled with still-warm shell casings. He had been "policing the range," walking around and cleaning up spent casings ejected from fired weapons. I understand that he didn't fire a single shot in his own defense.

Human beings are enormously complex animals, but stress can defeat us easily. When the situation is so overwhelming that we can no longer think effectively, we revert to simple muscle memory and gross motor skills. We do what we've been taught to do.

I stood over Mike's body for what seemed like an eternity. It took that long for me to understand that I could not repair this damage.

What shattering glass, flying steel, and the force of velocity can do to a human body is simply dumbfounding.

I remember that the smell of fuel blanketing the crash site was overwhelming.

I remember stumbling over a large piece of the fuselage.

I remember finding him.

It was obvious to me that he died quickly and did not suffer. I took his cooling hand in mine and told him I was sorry. There was nothing else I could do. I had finally encountered a problem I could not fix. I could not save my best friend.

An advisor from the LA Country Fire Department arrived on the scene next. He was disciplined in a way that surprised me. He insisted that nothing be touched. He sealed off the site and moved us away from the bodies of Mike Donatelli, David Gibbs, and cameraman Darren Rydstrom.

I remember sitting on the hillside with Dale as the sun rose and the details of the crash became evident to us. The helo went down hard, carving a long V-shaped trough through the dust and ancient silt of the lakebed. It must have nosed into the dirt under full power. The reasons are still unclear. The rotors, moving at several thousand miles per hour, had shattered and shredded the craft to a degree that made concrete findings extremely difficult.

Despite the darkness, I do not believe a veteran pilot like David Gibbs misjudged his altitude. I believe the accident was due to mechanical failure. It happened fast. Despite their bulk and solid appearance, helicopters are enormously complex and fragile vehicles subject to nearly unimaginable stresses. When they crash, they crash hard.

As the sun continued its slow ascent and the blackness of Sierra Pelona slowly receded, I thought back to the day before, a day that now seemed decades ago. It occurred to me that fate turns on the simplest factors. Mike was gone, and I wasn't. The reasons for it didn't include mechanical failure or pilot error. Instead, they boiled down to a simple choice and an oddball question.

Dale had spoken to us that morning, when the helicopter touched down. He had discussed the schedule with the pilot and then joined us at the Winnebago. He asked us a curious question, one that's damnably ironic, given the disaster that followed. He wondered out loud, "Who here has been in a helicopter crash?"

Dale had gone down in a helo in Panama and suffered a broken back when he was with Delta Force. Mike had survived a minor crash himself during a "capabilities exercise" when he was with the Rangers. I was the only one of our trio who had not had the absolute thrill of crashing and burning. So, I was more or less the obvious choice to fly first.

Mike and Dale discussed who would fly the second lift, and as fate would have it, Mike agreed to do the second run, unknowingly sparing Dale's life and mine. Had we chosen differently, Mike could have been the one on that dark hillside, scrambling to reach my body and fix it.

Sometimes life takes completely unexpected turns and there is virtually nothing you can do about it. No amount of preparation, training, muscle memory, armor, or hard-won expertise can help you. An old gunny I knew once told me, "You can train until you can swim like a fish, run like a jaguar, disassemble an M16 in thirty seconds, and build more muscle than Mr. Universe. But that crap doesn't matter. No amount of muscle ever stopped a bullet."

He left it right there. He didn't tell me what actually stops bullets. Kevlar comes to mind, but that isn't the right answer. Some might say being mentally prepared and thinking ahead is the best way to avoid absorbing a bullet. That's true on a certain level. But what the gunny was saying in his own peculiar way, by failing to provide an answer to the dilemma, is that often there is no answer. Life is unfair. Things go wrong. Bad things happen to good people. Sometimes there is nothing you can do to prevent your best friend from slipping away.

I sat on that hillside with Dale for hours, remembering Mike, trying hard to put dark thoughts aside and to recall the best parts of our relationship. I thank God for all the great memories I have of Mike. They have helped me tremendously since his death.

Mike had a wonderful sense of humor. We went through early

training together in Special Forces and then separated, each going to different units. We were finally reunited in Iraq, brothers in arms, deployed to kill bad guys. As we prepped for our first mission, Mike slapped my back and said eagerly, "Let's do this thing." Standing side by side with my best friend while fighting in Iraq is a memory I will cherish for the rest of my life and one of my most prized possessions.

That mission, as I remember, was a bust. Our target was warned, went to the ground, and escaped. When we returned to our compound, I noticed I was receiving plenty of awkward looks, smiles, and ribbing—a lot more than usual, actually. I have a big personality, and I don't make much of an effort to hide it. I tend to attract jokers and people determined to cut me down to size, as well as loyal, lifelong friends.

Eventually, someone removed the piece of paper taped to my back upon which Mike had scrawled, "Shoot me! I'm single."

I loved his sense of humor. He had a way of turning most situations around and finding the silver lining. I figured if he had been sitting on that hillside instead of me, he would have had Dale howling with laughter. He would have been filling his ears with embarrassing tales about good old Joe. He wouldn't have stopped until the tide went out, the waves of grief receded, and everyone was able to get back on their feet and function again. That was Mike.

But I'm not Mike. I wondered about his family. Mike had a very close-knit Italian family. He had five children who would now be fatherless. The news of Mike's death was going to break his wife's heart into pieces, and I doubted she would be able to put herself back together again, not for a long while.

My own feelings of guilt and responsibility were overwhelming. The gunny's words and his intent recurred to me again and again while I sat on that hill. It is a hard lesson to learn and harder still to accept. Some things cannot be changed or fixed. You simply have to deal with the consequences. How do you move on? How do get up and keep moving forward?

I dreaded the ordeal to come. A death in combat is expected. We accept the risk when we volunteer. Our safety is secondary to the mission, and everyone knows the drill. When you leave the confines of your compound, you know you might not be coming back. Because of that, there is sort of a cushion to losing a friend in battle. It's somehow more bearable. But losing a friend to a senseless, freak accident isn't so easy to explain away and compartmentalize.

At the time the brutal irony of the situation escaped me. That I had lost my best friend not to combat but to the filming of a reality show similar to the one for which I would soon become known was not on my mind.

All I could think about was Mike, his family's suffering, and how I was going to tell them that he was gone. How could I explain that their son, husband, father, and hero was never coming back?

Situational irony is defined as experiencing an outcome that is terribly different or at odds with the expected one. It is usually accompanied by sharp and remarkable contrasts, sometimes painful both emotionally and physically.

When John Hinckley attempted to assassinate Ronald Reagan, he got off six shots, and all of them missed the president. The sixth and last round, fired before the assassin was overcome, ricocheted off the bulletproof door of the limousine. Its trajectory was changed, and the slug found its intended victim. Reagan was badly wounded. Without the bulletproof armor, the president would have remained untouched. I don't think anyone saw that one coming.

Life is like that. The bad times, the ones that can rock you to your core and rattle the very foundations of your existence, are the ones you don't see coming. Life sometimes feels like a terrible cosmic joke, and the outcome is rarely what you expect. It's usually so twisted and bewildering that it easily qualifies as situational irony.

Mike's death was sudden and brutal. I was unable to prevent it. I wasn't sure that I was going to be able to move forward at all. Then the irony surfaced, as it always does. In that irony, I found hope and the necessary tools to heal.

At first, the head of the production company tasked with shooting the show wanted someone to call Mike's wife. I demanded that they send someone to the house personally to deliver the news; a phone call was not going to cut it. Mike and his family deserved so much better. I decided they deserved to hear it in person, as they would have if he'd perished in combat.

I cleaned myself up, made a few phone calls, and got in my car. I steeled myself to be the strong one, the shoulder to be cried on, and perhaps even the one to be blamed. I decided I could live with that. I felt then, and still do to a much lesser degree, that my decisions, like the bulletproof armor weighing down the president's limousine, had altered the trajectory of many lives forever.

Mike's family did not react as I expected. While they grieved for him and will always mourn his loss and the hole it left in their lives, they were not shell-shocked, beaten down, and fragile. They did not blame me. They did not question God. They did not turn inconsolable and cease to function. They did not lean on me for support and comfort. Instead, they opened their arms and hearts to me. I was the one who wound up looking to them for guidance and emotional reassurance.

I should have known. The family that produced a pillar of a man like Mike was unassailably strong at its core and loving beyond my experience. Mike's adventurous career and past brushes with death simply made them more so. He welded them into a loving unit capable of withstanding anything, even his sudden passing. Mike had done the hard work of building a real, loving family, even while he was away and risking himself to preserve a future for them. There is no better testament to him than the family he left behind. Their outreach to me was wonderful, warm, and amazing. They took me in. They shared their love and faith, their grief and strength.

I lost my mother early on. I grew up lonely. It took my best friend's passing to give me an amazing gift—an introduction to a sort of familial bond that I never knew existed—and it made me begin to think seriously about building my own family. There is a lot of irony in Mike's death. He certainly would have appreciated it.

Despite the randomness of the accident that claimed Mike, specific lessons can be learned from it, from my reaction, and from the startling response of his family to the terrible wound that was inflicted on them.

A true survivor always takes stock, learns what he or she can from unfolding events, and uses that information in future endeavors. That it took such an unspeakable tragedy like Mike's passing to get me to look back and truly examine my life is a bitter pill to swallow.

But human beings are naturally shortsighted. As a rule, we don't realize what we have until it's gone. Nor do we forgive ourselves easily. Nor do we willingly get up and walk forward.

I think about Mike often. Almost daily I would get my six a.m. wakeup call from him. I know he wouldn't have chosen such a death or leaving his family at that point in time if given the option. But I know somewhere, somehow, he is pleased. I'm sure he takes comfort in the noble life he led and how even his absence has had a profound and inspiring effect on those he cared for.

He changed the course of my life without any doubt. In death, he gave me the greatest gift I have ever received. He spurred me to think hard about the future and what I really wanted to accomplish before my own passing. Most importantly, he granted me the opportunity to appreciate just how far I've come—and to contemplate what might have been and what could still be if I made the right choices.

So much in life hinges on those little choices. While sitting on that hillside I thought about my childhood and how much had resulted from my boyhood dreams and decisions.

5

CRAWL, WALK, RUN

"My childhood did not prepare me for the fact that the
world is full of cruel and bitter things."

—J. ROBERT OPPENHEIMER

THE PENNSYLVANIA SUBURBS—THE 1970S
THE MAKING OF A COMMANDO (PART 1)

I GREW UP AN ONLY child, in a suburb of Pittsburgh, Pennsylvania, called Turtle Creek. I can tell you that my upbringing wasn't easy. I was deeply lonely. I often prayed for God to send me a brother or a sister. It didn't happen. By the time I started school, my parents were barely on speaking terms. Shortly after my seventh birthday, they divorced.

My father's family hailed from Palermo, Sicily. My mother's people came from Croatia. I didn't know much about my mother's relatives. My dad's large, extended family was a constant presence in our lives. For a while there, I was convinced that I was 100 percent Italian.

Sunday dinners were a rotating affair, held at the homes of different family members from week to week. In the warm and familiar Catholic Italian tradition, we gathered most often at my grandmother's house. I would come to live there later, following the traumatic collapse of my parents' long-suffering marriage.

My grandmother could throw together a spaghetti dinner like no one else. To this day I haven't enjoyed pasta as good as hers. Her noodles were homemade, and the red sauce came from canned tomatoes that she grew herself in a backyard garden. I will never forget the smell of those wonderful Sunday suppers.

As the family arrived at my grandmother's home, the genders split, bent on different missions. The guys headed for the front room to watch sports on the big console television that dominated the space. The women disappeared into the kitchen to help with the cooking and gossip.

My male cousins were big Steelers and Pirates fans. I didn't much care about "roided-up," overpaid athletes knocking each other around for several hours at a stretch. To this day I can't tell you how many guys are on a football team. Organized sports have never appealed to me. I was a poor athlete at best as a kid. I was almost always the last kid chosen for pickup baseball games and dodgeball death matches. I was skinny and subject to a lot of ribbing about my size and lack of musculature. I had little to no confidence in my physical abilities.

Most of my friends were pretty good at one sport or another—baseball, basketball, hockey, or football, generally. Some were natural, gifted athletes who could play them all, like my buddy Tim. There was only one thing that I was good at and confident in doing. I enjoyed playing in the woods at night. That sounds odd now, even to me. In those days I wasn't exactly the poster boy for bravery. But I was comfortable in the darkness. I could hide among the silent, uncaring trees and bushes. I could create my own adventures and worlds. No one called me skinny. No one laughed about my inability to throw a baseball. My parents' arguments faded away, and I could no longer hear their injured, angry voices.

If you were to ask me today why my parents divorced, I would tell you it boiled down to a lack of money. Period. So many thorny incompatibilities and issues had grown up between them over the years that their quarrels were baffling, circling, repeating, expletive-laced tirades without end or resolution. Their marriage was an ugly battlefield pockmarked by arguments like landing exploding shells. Money, and the lack thereof, was always a factor. It wasn't the only issue of course, but it was certainly the one that provoked the most violent and contentious arguments. They couldn't pay the bills. It was hard to put food on the table. The lack of cash strained them both to the breaking point.

I was raised in a poor household. I am not ashamed to admit that. There were times when we had no electricity. I remember a cold winter day when there was no heat in the house. I could see my breath. I might as well have been outside in the snow for all the good those four walls did me. I remember licking and pasting S&H Green Stamps into my mother's coupon books. She could buy necessary household items with those stamps at a deep discount. I remember my parents using food stamps to buy food. Without them, there would have been nothing to eat in our house. I raided a local Goodwill box for my school clothes. My good buddy Tim would hold my legs while I fished out clothes with a metal hanger. One night I struck gold and scored a pair of Jordache jeans that fit! I remember my excitement at the find. I was nearly delirious.

My father did his best, but he was frequently unemployed. Jobs were scarce in those days, particularly for a man who had no college education and lacked particular skills. He worked in sales mostly. He was unsalaried and lived and died on commission. He was a good man and an honest human being. He tried hard to provide for us. But he failed more often than he succeeded. It wasn't really his fault. Sometimes, most of the time really, life is unfair. The universe doesn't cooperate with us. The "why" doesn't matter. Those heated arguments between my parents were superfluous. They didn't change a thing, and all the harsh words tore my loving mother and father apart.

Growing up with no money traumatized me, and I'm affected by it to this day. The effects and the fear of poverty hit me at a gut level. My friends will tell you that Joe has ZERO sense of humor when it comes to money. They will add that Joe can't step over a penny on the ground. He'll pick up the nearly worthless coin and keep it, every time. They'll then quote the phrase I utter most often: "There is no nobility in poverty." Finally, they'll explain to you that Joe wouldn't change a thing about his background or difficult childhood. That's true. My experiences made me who I am today. I'm proud of the man I became and every one of my accomplishments.

I am a survivor. Growing up around poverty hardened me at a young age. I learned early that if I wanted a particular thing, I was going to have to get it myself. I will do what's necessary to survive and prosper. I owe my success to the failures of my parents and ultimately to their damaged love for one another and me. Odd motivations, but very effective.

When I was in school, my dearest friend was Tim. We grew up just down the road from one another. We were bonded from the start. Our friendship remained alive right into adulthood. We are close to this day, despite years apart and careers that grew in different directions.

Tim's childhood was as harsh as mine but for different reasons. His stepfather, Dave, was a Korean War veteran and a prisoner of war for two hellish years. He was a decent man, but his torturers had harmed him in ways that exceeded the effects of physical trauma. He was broken spiritually and mentally. His reactions to the world around him were surprising and sometimes difficult to understand. I get it now. I didn't then. Due to my association with the military and my preference for friends who've served, I've come to recognize the symptoms of PTSD (post-traumatic stress disorder). I've seen the damaging effects on combat survivors and their families over and over. In the 1970s there was no help or hope for a man like Dave. Tim caught the full brunt of his stepfather's outbursts and mental illness.

Dave placed a lock on the family refrigerator. Tim could only eat when he finished his chores and his stepfather approved of the work he'd done. Only then did the key come out. To earn a bologna sandwich, Tim washed the dishes, hauled the trash outside, and mopped the floor. This ritual occurred every night without fail. If Tim didn't perform a task to his stepfather's excruciating standards, or failed to display proper humility, or didn't move quickly enough, he went hungry for a long time. You can't make this sort of thing up. Witnessing my best friend's suffering was emotionally numbing.

When Tim was thirteen, he made a small, perfectly understandable mistake and ended up grounded for the entire summer. It was an unjust punishment. It was ridiculous, really. As his friend, I couldn't bear the thought of him sitting in his room while the rest of us were out running the fields, screaming our fool heads off, playing under sprinklers, or biking up and down the roads like we owned them. I was angry that Tim was his stepfather's whipping post. I couldn't do much about their relationship. But what I could do was comfort my best friend.

I spent that summer indoors with Tim. We sat at the kitchen table all day long in full view of the locked refrigerator. We played chess and Monopoly, game after game, for three solid months. We talked a lot about what we would do when we were grown and free.

Not long ago Tim and I were sharing some memories over the phone. He said something that really struck me. He mentioned his stepfather. Then he said, "Joe, I never thanked you for spending that summer with me when I was grounded. You don't know what that meant to me."

At the time I didn't consider how I was affecting anyone. I felt for my friend, and I detested his stepfather's behavior. It was a little thing, really. It was easier for me to be with Tim than in my own home, a place filled with loss, anger, stress, and truly awful emotions. Now and then I am amazed at the effects of our inconsequential decisions upon others. I never considered that my small action had such a profound impact on my friend. In reflecting on that conversation, I became convinced that the smallest decisions we make while we walk the path of life have the most far-reaching consequences, like ripples in a pond expanding outward. Throughout the years the results of those decisions come back to us in different ways, some positive and some hauntingly negative. We can find ourselves pinned into a corner and at the mercy of our earlier judgment calls and stupid mistakes.

We can't change the past, but what we can do is make good and informed decisions. Additionally, it doesn't hurt to be kind to someone you meet along the path who is clearly suffering. I gained a lifelong friend by sacrificing my freedom for a summer. I couldn't ask for a better return. To this day Tim is a constant inspiration for me and a true blessing in my life.

I'll add this. Do not fall into the "what if" trap. Continually reflecting on your failures and indulging in reveries about changing the past is useless. Worse, such thinking will consume every bit of your mental energy and will throw you into a cycle of depression that's difficult to break. I do not play the "what if" game. It's healthy to think about and learn from your mistakes so that you don't repeat them, but doing so to excess leads to illness and yet more failure. This is another negative feedback loop that must be avoided, similar in many ways to the "why me" question discussed in Chapter Three.

With that in mind, I will talk about my mother. Remembering her now, nearly forty years after her passing, brings tears to my eyes. The pain of her loss still hurts me to my core. Contrary to what you might think, I do have fond memories of my youth. Almost all of them involve my mother in some way. She was what a parent should be. She was supportive when I needed it most. She was critical of my actions when I needed it most. She encouraged me to dream. She urged me to follow my dreams and build the life that I wanted.

Most importantly, when I fell, she didn't pick me up. She made me pick myself up. She loved me unconditionally with all her heart. And I knew it.

I knew from a very early age I wanted to join the military. I planned to do so immediately after high school. I set my sights on the Marine Corps. My mother supported that decision. Some members of my family did not. They were critical of me, remarking on my poor athletic skills and unimpressive physique. They said I wouldn't survive Marine Corps boot camp and that the disappointment over my failure would crush me.

They were critical of my mother. They felt she was wrong to encourage her child to go down such a risky path. She didn't care what they thought or said about her after the divorce. My mother kept me focused on my goals. Her encouragement was what propelled me to excel, to build a career that placed me at the tip of the spear in a special operations unit during a critical phase in our nation's history.

I was in eleventh grade when my mother passed away. It was a sudden thing. It was a gut-wrenching experience that left me adrift and feeling lost for years. People die. I'm sure you've heard all the trite aphorisms, such as "She's not suffering anymore," "She's in heaven now," "Thank goodness it was quick," "We all have to go sometime," and on and on and on. Yes, people die. But the ones closest to you are not simply "people." They are your guides and mentors and spiritual overseers, and they teach you what love is and what it can be. They are such a critical part of you that the wide hole left in your body by their passing is unfillable. It is like losing every limb. You are never whole again. You can't be. The most essential part of you is missing, and it can't be regained.

I've never felt such heavy, crushing grief. I had no time to process what was coming. She was there, and then she was gone. I cannot say whether it's better to lose a loved one without warning or to watch them pass slowly. In the latter case, you do have the time to tell them how much you love them and clear the air of many things.

In the former case, my mother's case, there is no suffering and no opportunity to say your goodbyes.

I was inconsolable. I had lost the one person who encouraged me to pursue my dreams and dreamed right along with me. My mother was the person who sparked my interest in the outdoors. She had taken me shooting and bow hunting. She helped me purchase my first bow, a Bear Grizzly forty-five-pound recurve that we discovered together at a yard sale. We couldn't afford any repairs or accessories. The pin sight was missing. I used Scotch tape to affix a nail to the grip, which was surprisingly effective. I took my first deer with that ancient, weather-beaten bow. I was endlessly inventive in the quest to improve my archery skills. I went through the neighbors' garbage cans on trash day, searching for stuffed animals to use as 3-D targets. I built a righteous collection of fluffy targets that ranged from skunks to giraffes. Train as you will fight, I always say! To my surprise, I became quite an accomplished archer at a very young age.

My mother's sister Katherine had a home in Butler County that she shared with her husband, Walter. Some of my most cherished childhood memories spring from the time spent at that place, which verged on thick forest. It was there that I learned to hunt. It was there that I bagged my first deer using that old bow.

I remember waking up before the sunrise. I made my way outside and to a tree stand that my cousin and I had constructed. The stand overlooked a field overgrown by rye grass and dotted with crabapple trees. A small creek ran through the place. It was a textbook feeding ground for deer.

When the rising sun peeked through the trees, I watched the field in front of me take shape and materialize out of the darkness. I remember thinking that I was in for a very long day. I saw myself in my mind, at sunset, dragging my first deer across the fields to Aunt Katherine and Uncle Walter's home. As it turned out, my wait was short. A mere two hours passed, and then I saw a muscular five-point buck working his way through the rye grass and searching for fallen crabapples. I struck him down at forty yards with my yard-sale recurve bow. It was an amazing shot, and one that I will never forget. Believe it or not, I still have the arrow that dropped him.

That bow now hangs on the wall in my gear room. I haven't shot it since high school. It would probably shatter if I applied forty-five pounds of torque to the aging hardwood frame. But I value it highly and will never let go of it. It is one of my most prized possessions. There are other objects on that wall that bring me pleasure, but the bow provides me the most joy. It is a material connection to my mother. I can only hope she hears my continuous thanks for all the support and love she gave me. I'd like to believe that she's proud of the man I've become. I learned so many life lessons from my mother. We forged wonderful memories together. Sometimes, when I touch that bow, I can feel her presence.

My advice to you is not to turn away from your past. It's to embrace what you were, understand your failures, celebrate even your smallest successes, and cherish the few mementoes that accompany you into the future, that aren't lost on the long and winding road. These objects are the fuel that drives us to succeed and perform at optimal levels. They are the visual motivations that made it possible for an ordinary man like me to do extraordinary things. They are anchors that keep us grounded. They are spiritual connections to those who went before us and guided us on the right path. They are our support in times of crisis.

A crisis can take many forms. It might surprise you to know that I was severely bullied in high school. Due to my slight size and polite nature, I was an easy target. One particular fellow enjoyed making my life miserable. I won't call him out by name here. It's been a few years since we last encountered each other. I believe he still lives in the old neighborhood. I'd like to think he's taken the time to get his life together and now helps where he used to hurt.

For argument's sake, we'll call him Robert. Robert was angry. I never discovered what caused his rage. I don't particularly care.

Every morning he arrived at the bus stop early and staked out the territory as if it was his personal hunting ground. I was his prey of choice. The bullying took many forms. He'd steal my backpack and/or my milk money. When I didn't give them up willingly, he'd deliver a beatdown that left me bruised and dirty.

He was a fan of televised studio wrestling, the fake sort with highly choreographed moves that no street brawler would dare use in a fight. Trying those silly dance routines on just about any enemy would have earned you a serious ass whipping. Striking a karate pose and yelling, "Hiya!" would have been more effective than a Gorgeous George corkscrew elbow drop. But Robert adored those moves. He used them all on me—chokeholds, headlocks, short-arm smashes, forearm chops, and flying leg drops, always followed by the dreaded sleeper hold.

It got so bad that I began hiding around the corner at the firehouse. I would run out and leap aboard when the school bus was loaded.

The bullying went on for three years. He harassed me from the start of my sophomore year until I graduated. I'm certain I suffered an early bout of PTSD due to his bullying and the violence he dished out. I had nightmares about him for years. I was tortured by these visions into early adulthood. Not even my first stint in the Marine Corps nor my growing physical strength and self-confidence dismissed them. Only time, plenty of distance, and life and death encounters with real and capable enemies made them fade. I replaced Robert with new monsters.

Everyone gets bullied, even the bullies. But we shouldn't dismiss the pain or make light of the suffering. Physical and emotional violence are real, and the damage these do to a human being can last forever. I'm going to make a point in a moment. It applies mostly to the bullies, but their victims are included in the message. What you read next may shock you. But remember, there is a lesson to be learned and absorbed in what occurred next.

Three decades passed, and I put Robert behind me. I endured four years in the Marine Corps, nine in Special Forces, and qualified for and worked with an elite counterterrorist unit that operated off the grid, employing the most feared warriors in the world. I was quite capable of handling myself at that point. I was no longer a ninety-nine-pound weakling.

One summer I went home to see my father. He had fallen and broken his hip. I thought it might be one of the last visits we had. It was June in Pittsburgh, and the early summer days were already hot and muggy. I woke up one morning and decided to go for a run. I dressed appropriately for the weather. I threw on running shoes and a pair of shorts. I planned to jog down to a bridge in downtown Turtle Creek, turn around at the main intersection, and return home, a round-trip excursion of about three miles. It was an easy run. I didn't want to be challenged that morning.

When I reached the turnaround point in Turtle Creek, I stopped. I'm not sure why I did that. I must have felt something in the air. For reasons that I still can't explain, I crossed four lanes of highway traffic and trotted down a long sidewalk that ran past a small shopping center. I glanced into a coffee shop window. I saw three men sitting in a booth. I recognized only one, Robert.

The dreams of Robert had stopped long before. I honestly believed I held no ill will toward him. But the sight of my old antagonist and torturer threw me. An unbelievable fury rose up in my chest, a swelling hatred that I couldn't contain. I found it hard to breathe. My blood began to boil. My rage was uncontrollable.

I threw open the door, stormed into the restaurant, and went straight to Robert's booth. I was covered in sweat and layered slabs of muscle. I was now a 199-pound mass of pure rage, with a deadly set of skills honed over many years. I recalled everything he had done to me in a moment while he sat and stared at me with wide eyes. He knew me at once. And he was afraid. I saw it in his eyes.

I asked, "Do you remember me?"

He didn't answer. His lower lip quivered.

I pushed my way into the booth. I shoved him aside with my hip and went face-to-face with the bully who had haunted my dreams and still had a place in the darkest part of my soul.

I said, "You know, Robert, I really hated the way you treated me in high school. As a matter of fact, I had bad dreams about what you did to me. The dreams lasted for years."

Robert's response was typical of a bully. It was delivered without thought or apology. On a level, I expected it. He replied in a dismissive voice, "Hey, man, I was just messing around."

The beatings had been one thing. That was bad enough. But the pain he had inflicted hadn't been sufficient to satisfy him. After a little while, he had added psychological torture to his wrestling moves. In high school, he called my father a "deadbeat and a loser." He had said no one respected the man. He spoke frequently and badly of my dead mother. He used words to describe her that I cannot repeat. At the time I couldn't stop him. My helplessness never gave him pause. It just gave him pleasure.

Now his blasé attitude about the pain he had inflicted enraged me further. It was all I could do not to drag him outside and beat the man to death.

Sensing that things were spinning out of control, one of his friends asked, "Hey, man. Who are you? You looking for trouble?" Perhaps he thought I would be intimidated by the weak, tacked-on, and implicit threat. I wasn't.

I'm told I get crazy eyes when I'm angry, like Charles Manson. I must have gotten them then because I turned my head and he began to squirm. I said, "If you want to stay healthy, you need to sit there and keep your mouth shut." He looked down at the table and didn't offer another word in his friend's defense. Bullies don't have real friends. They're followed around by like kind. And they never have your back.

I fastened my gaze on Robert again. I asked, "Do you remember all those wrestling moves you used to get me in? Why don't you try that shit on me now?"

His response was lame. He said simply, "No thanks."

I broke then. The dam burst. My rage and all that suppressed pain came flooding back and swept away my self-control. The genie was out of the bottle and there was no putting him back. I grabbed Robert by the shirt collar and hauled him outside. I took a personal interest in seeing him suffer . . . in a big way. He didn't walk away from his latest fight with good old Joe. He departed in an ambulance and lay in a hospital bed for two weeks.

It wasn't right. I shouldn't have done it. I'm not proud of myself. There could have been serious legal consequences, and quite frankly, I could have killed him. But Robert didn't press charges. He understood that I had let him off lightly. He knew that I could have turned out his lights permanently. As I said before, I hope he turned his life around and attempted to make amends with the many people he had injured down through the years. I hope that beating was some kind of watershed moment for him.

Now to the point. The point is directed at the bullies, whether you are sixteen and consider a school bus stop your hunting ground, or you're a fifty-five-year-old boss who terrorizes his employees, or you happen to be a mujahedeen fighter squatting in a cave with visions of the apocalypse dancing around and around in your brain. You should be careful about who you harass, intimidate, and hurt. As they say, karma is a bitch. It might take thirty years, but she *will* come back around to bite you for all you've done. The evil you dish out *will* catch up to you. When it happens, maybe I'll be there to assist karma and speed up the lesson. That's all I have to say on the matter.

6

NO MORE
WOODEN GUNS

"Let us form one body, one heart, and defend to the last
warrior our country, our homes, our liberty, and
the graves of our fathers."

—TECUMSEH

THE MAKING OF A COMMANDO (PART 2)

ONE OF MY FAVORITE places to play as a kid was the Union
Railroad roundhouse. This massive building was located in a muddy
yard crisscrossed by rusting tracks. The place lay four miles from
my home, which was a fair distance when you were forced to hike
or bike it.

My friend Tim and I kept the place a closely guarded secret for
a while. Later we invited a neighbor named Bill to join us at our
makeshift "commando training center." It was the hub of operations,
out of which we ran dozens of successful covert missions against
imaginary targets.

I dreamed of being a commando. I had a subscription to *Soldier of Fortune* magazine. I read it religiously, absorbing every detail I could about mercenaries, high-powered weapons, and the African continent, where whole nations and vast fortunes always teetered in the balance. I enjoyed other military-themed rags, but none had *SOF's* exciting prose, bold photos, and shockingly detailed descriptions of paramilitary operations. The epic successes and failures of the adventurous men described in those pages fascinated me to no end.

A vision took root in my mind. I saw myself in jungle fatigues crossing exotic landscapes in hot pursuit of the bad guys. I wanted that future. I wanted to be a commando more than anything else. I learned from the pages of those magazines that there are certain steps one has to take in order to succeed at the dream.

I remember the magazine that sparked my initial interest in the Marine Corps and my eventual decision to join up. It was called *Gung-Ho*, which actually means "working together." I learned that in Marine boot camp, much later. *Gung-Ho* wasn't as sporty or glamorous as *SOF*, but it was gritty and real. The cover photo of that particular issue featured a Marine Recon team standing around their IBS (inflatable boot small), all camouflaged up. The feature article on Marine Recon teams turned my head. The writer's superb prose and praise for the Marines was the primary influence that set me on a winding, dangerous career path that lasted more than twenty years.

I was determined to succeed at my dream. I refused to smoke or do drugs. I felt those things would compromise my body and render me unfit for the service. I avoided trouble. I worked just hard enough to earn average grades and graduate from high school. The Marines required a high school diploma. I was determined to get one, but not to work too hard at it. I was not a bad student, just one that didn't apply himself or study.

The Union Railroad roundhouse gave me the perfect opportunity to hone my skills as a "wannabe" commando. While I towed the line and obeyed the rules almost without fail, I was operating in a gray area when it came to the roundhouse. The roundhouse and the yard were private property, heavily patrolled by Union Railroad security. The facility was lit up like a Christmas tree at night. It looked like a prison, complete with a guard tower and armed, hulking defenders both on foot and in vehicles.

Tim was busy most nights, satisfying his stepfather's demands and trying hard to earn a meal. Bill was free to come and go. I'd known Bill since the fourth grade. Inviting him to train with me at the roundhouse was a no-brainer. I trusted him completely, and he shared my love of the woods and the military.

Bill's family was kind to me. I felt like I belonged when I was in his house, among his brothers and sharing a dinner at their table. I spent more nights sleeping at Bill's place than I can remember. We often sneaked out of his bedroom window at midnight and beelined across a mile of woods to reach the roundhouse. We weren't playing. We were running missions, meticulously detailed operations taken straight from the pages of the *U.S. Army Ranger Handbook*. We were serious about those ops. We studied that manual like a playbook for a professional football team.

Ironically, I attended more than thirty schools while serving in special operations. Ranger School wasn't one of them. Go figure.

Each of us had a copy of the *U.S. Army Ranger Handbook*. We followed the five-paragraph Operations Orders in that book to the letter. Bill and I would write out the mission a week in advance. We had a little ISOFAC (isolation facility) set up in his bedroom closet. We sealed ourselves in and worked by the light of a Coleman lantern to draft op orders. We worked in secret and used code names to disguise our plans. Then we'd wait patiently for Saturday to roll around. Saturday was "execution day."

We called the Union Railroad "The Spider's Web." It looked like a web due to the crisscrossing tracks. There was a washed-out wooden bridge about a mile from the roundhouse. We called it "The Halfway Point." No points for imagination there. We weren't military planners, though we wanted to be. We took those missions seriously. They had an impact on me that would last a lifetime. I was thinking in a tactical manner at a very young age. That sort of discipline is hard for adults to muster, but I was doing well at it at twelve years old. Thank you, *U.S. Army Ranger Handbook.*

Ralph's Army Surplus was located near my home. I spent a lot of time at that store. As of the writing of this book, Ralph's is still open. I have to admit, tears came to my eyes when I Googled the name and their website popped up. The memories I have of those days growing up have always given me a good feeling and an incredible sense of accomplishment.

I purchased my "kit" for the Union Railroad missions at Ralph's. I paid for the gear by cutting grass and shoveling snow. The so-called "kit" wasn't particularly fancy. My first gear purchase included an old-school Vietnam era H-harness with all the bells and whistles. I had two M14 ammo pouches, two canteens, a canvas butt pack, and a Buck knife my grandfather had given me for my birthday the year before. Later I snagged a pair of old school jungle boots and a boonie hat.

What I didn't have was a cool set of BDUs (battle dress uniforms). The smallest sizes made were far too large and baggy for my small frame. Instead, I bought a one-piece kiddie camouflage jumpsuit at Sears. Bill busted my chops about it constantly. It was a source of great amusement for him. But I made do. I got by. A commando has to use any available tools to fulfill his mission.

The final missing piece of my kit was the most critical to the mission. I didn't have a gun. Needless to say, at my young age I wasn't about to lay hands on a genuine M16 or even a Daisy BB Gun. But I was endlessly resourceful. My grandfather was a skilled carpenter. I asked if he could make a gun for me out of wood. He agreed without hesitation. I drew the weapon carefully on a long sheet of paper, studying an image in a *Soldier of Fortune* magazine as I worked. I wanted to make sure he got the measurements right.

The result was beyond my expectations. I painted my spiffy new M16 black and used some of my grandmother's clothesline twine as a sling. I was in business.

I would push my Harley-Davidson off a cliff if I could get that gun back today. I treasured it. Sadly, it vanished along with all my hard-earned gear when I left for Marine Corps boot camp.

Our Union Railroad missions were simple at first. We would leave Bill's house, patrol through the woods, practice being quiet, and sit on the hill facing the facility. We observed the train yard and main facility for hours. We took extensive notes on what we saw, what time the trains pulled out, when they arrived, what time the security vehicle came around, how many people we saw, and where and when we saw them. To this day I am staggered by the level of detail in the notes we took and how careful and meticulous we were in inscribing our findings. We had plenty of practice. We began our missions as early as the seventh grade, utilizing tactics learned from our trusty *Ranger* manuals.

It was not long until Bill and I became bored. Performing "recon" on the Union Railroad was easy now. We decided it was time to stretch our wings and take it to the next level.

I remember saying to Bill one day after school, "Ya know, Bill, I bet you we could sneak into the Spider's Web without anyone seeing us. How much you wanna bet?" I could tell from Bill's big smile that he was all over it. We began planning our raid the same day.

I have to say, this is where we stepped over the line. This is when we crossed over into the morally gray area I mentioned earlier. The roundhouse and surrounding buildings were private property. Plenty of posted signs made this perfectly clear. We were on the verge of taking a VERY big step, one that could have had serious repercussions. We were kids of course. That might have earned us a little slack. But getting busted sneaking around at two o'clock in the morning dressed up in military camo wasn't going to turn out well any way you sliced it.

We didn't take the time to discuss the implications or perform a risk assessment. Like most kids, we were ignorant of greater dangers and their consequences.

Our new mission had no name in the 1975 version of the *Ranger* handbook. In the years to come I would learn that the military dubbed it a CTR (close target reconnaissance).

Our plan was relatively complex, and the holes in it weren't immediately evident to us. After all, we were junior high kids with no real-world experience in covert ops.

It was Bill who gamed out the CTR and came up with a working plan. We intended to approach the roundhouse via a concrete tunnel that diverted a small creek. The tunnel was high enough for us to walk through. The water in the creek ranged in depth from a few inches to three feet. We would follow the creek and exit the water about 100 meters from the main building. There we would halt, since the lights were bright and glaring beyond this point. The creek approach included the only semidark area on the entire property. We would wait for the guards to turn away then run the short distance to the roundhouse wall. Once against the wall, we would quickly peek into the roundhouse and observe what we could. Mission accomplished.

Considering our age and the fact we were teaching ourselves how to think tactically, it was amazing that we did so well. The two *Ranger* manuals and that stack of *SOF* magazines were our bibles. We learned everything we could from those publications. By the time we attempted our first risky mission, we knew we were ready.

We got the "go" on a warm summer night. Bill wanted to crash at my house and walk down the railroad tracks to the target. The first obstacle we ran into was presented by my dad. He was up late that night. He never went to bed without looking in on me. Leaving the house while he was awake would have been a bad move. The television was on downstairs. We read our magazines, perched on the end of my bed, and waited anxiously for the muddled talk and music to cease.

He finally threw in the towel at around one in morning. He clumped up the stairs and popped open my door. I remember thinking that he didn't look well. His face was drawn, and he seemed anxious. He asked, "You guys going to sleep?"

I told him we were going to stay up and watch television. He nodded and headed off to bed. We waited half an hour, giving him plenty of time to fall into a deep slumber. We sortied from base late, at 0145. We put on our gear, slipped through my bedroom window, made for the woods, and followed the railroad tracks to our objective.

Bill had a watch and was our official timekeeper. At precisely 0300 we arrived at the bridge that overlooked the Union Railroad yard. Immediately we realized there was a second serious hitch in our plan. Five sets of railroad tracks separated us from the creek and concrete tunnel. The tracks were lit up by floodlights mounted on the bridge and roundhouse. They were easily observable from any angle.

Because we were inexperienced, we chose to ignore the longer, safer approach. We should have moved along the wood line to the creek and waded in from there. Instead, we decided to dash across the tracks as fast as we could. The benefit, we felt, was in the timing. The track approach would take thirty seconds. The safer route would take a full thirty minutes, which I found unacceptable.

We had carefully selected our route from the water to the roundhouse as it was not well lit and offered us concealment while moving from the water to the building. What we didn't know was that there were motion sensors attached to the huge floodlights covering the area. Attention to detail was not one of our skill sets. Nor did we have a good grasp of modern security protocols and equipment. I had no idea that motion sensors existed.

As we approached the roundhouse, three massive floods popped on. We might as well have been in a baseball stadium lit up for a night game. We were fully exposed. The mission was blown. I was scared to death, worried about the consequences and sure we were trapped.

Then I heard Bill yell, "RUN!"

I hadn't considered the possibility, but it occurred to me that he had the right idea. It was then that I experienced my first adrenaline dump. It wouldn't be the last by far. I leapt and ran, heading for the darkness and the woods. I tripped all over myself. I stumbled through the creek and heard my panicked gasps echoing off the walls of the concrete tunnel. I ran blindly into the sheltering trees, bounced off several, lost sight of Bill, and headed down the rusty old tracks toward home at a gallop.

I made it back before sunrise. I was soaking wet and shaking like a leaf when I arrived. I was worried about Bill. But he was clever. He had taken the short route, right back to his house. He called me later to confirm that he was safe. I had run three miles. He had run one. He was asleep in his own bed long before I saw mine. I felt like a complete idiot.

Now most kids would have called it quits at that point. We had narrowly escaped discovery and capture. We had failed miserably despite our meticulously detailed plan. But we looked at it as a learning opportunity filled with additional challenges. The Union Railroad roundhouse was proving a tough nut to crack. We struggled to find a workable solution and came up empty.

The answer to our dilemma proved to be deceptively simple. We needed more information. The *Ranger* manual wasn't cutting it anymore. That meant we needed to find brand new sources of data. In the disco dancing '70s there was no Internet. Jumping online and digging up a cool military manual was not an option. There was only one place to go for what we needed: good old Ralph's Army Surplus.

We pedaled our bikes up to Ralph's that weekend, looking for new reading material that would help us accomplish our new goal of getting up close and personal with the Union Railroad.

Bill had just celebrated his birthday and had a few bucks to spend. Ralph's had devoted an entire wall of the store to military literature. If there was a military manual available for public dissemination, the store had it. If they didn't have a proper copy, they had a bootleg version of the book in question. We were dumbfounded by what we saw, mostly because we had never noticed the books before. For such observant kids, we had definite blind spots.

We purchased a knock-off version of the Army's *Special Forces Handbook* ST31-180 as well as several others. We also bought a small canvas backpack and two inert "pineapple grenades" of WWII vintage.

One of the manuals we purchased was a blessing and curse at the same time. It made us think about things that hadn't crossed our minds at such tender ages. It pushed us hard and sent us stumbling like fools right into the gray area. Before I go any further, please note that we never stole anything or caused actual property damage. The only thing we could have been accused of was trespassing and stupidity, lots and lots of stupidity. We were kids exploring a fantasy about being commandos. We weren't criminals.

We pushed on, determined to overcome the obstacles that had prevented us from completing our mission. It was the "never quit, let's figure out how to do this" attitude that would be my salvation in the difficult years to come. It is my opinion that you are born with the ability to persevere or it's missing from your DNA. I exhibited unusual stubbornness and tenacity at a young age. Once I started something, I finished it. Granted, I was not an athlete, nor did I excel at school. I was passionate about one thing: I wanted to serve my country on the battlefield. I wanted to stand alongside the most elite and daring soldiers in the history of human warfare. I did all those things. I found a way despite my shortcomings. That is the very definition of perseverance.

Bill and I read the manuals over the course of the next week. We learned new methods of planning and observation. We learned when to back down, abort the mission, and rethink our strategy. It didn't take long to deduce that collecting more information about the target was key. More data equaled a better chance of success.

Bill and I agreed that we were lucky that morning. We hadn't gotten caught, which would have put a permanent end to our missions. Our heads were filled with new tactics. We struggled a find a way to fit them all together. We understood the basic principles, but we couldn't see how they meshed. We weren't able to imagine a grand strategy based on the knowledge contained in that jumble of manuals and dry military text.

What the manuals did do was make us cocky, not confident. We had stumbled upon a treasure trove of knowledge. Never mind the fact that we didn't really understand what we were reading. We felt different and surer of ourselves. We were in a brand-new class. We were *real* commandos. We took it to a new level. We pushed the envelope. Sometimes a little push is all you need.

We ran new missions. Not only were we able to approach the Union Railroad without compromise or setting off the lights, we were able to gain access to any part of the structure we wanted while the mechanics were working on the trains.

One particular mission proved to me that I was meant to do this kind of work. While on a previous foray to the roundhouse, we entered the building from a side door that faced a parking lot. We discovered the locker room where the mechanics changed their clothing.

We spent no more than a minute in the room and left, but while there I got a close look at one of the mechanic's uniforms. The one-piece suit was on a coat hanger, dangling from a door handle on the outside of a locker. The employees of the roundhouse wore dark-blue jumpsuits with an embossed Union Railroad logo on the left breast pocket. They wore name tags pinned to the right breast pocket. An idea sprang into my mind. I stood there staring at the uniform for a few precious seconds. Then Bill shook me out of my daze, and we left in a hurry.

We had the roundhouse wired for sound. We knew every door, whether it was locked or left unlocked, when the shift change happened, and how many guys filled out each shift. We knew where the guard shack was, where the security vehicles were parked, how many were in the motor pool, and even the license plate numbers of the individual cruisers.

My idea was bold, and it took us into uncharted waters. It was dangerous, and it left no room for error. Either we would succeed or fail completely. Failure meant that one of us would be captured. We had no idea what interrogation methods were used by the Union Railroad against spies. But we knew it would only be a matter of time before the captured commando cracked and revealed the identity of the second man.

My idea was as simple as it was outlandish. I proposed sneaking one of us into the roundhouse, into the main work area. That infiltrator would hide and count name tags. He would also collect the descriptions of every mechanic and supervisor that he could fit in his head.

Over the course of the next few weeks we labored over our mission plan. We argued about who would attempt that suicidal foray into enemy territory. I was concerned about my future. I felt certain that failure would cost me any shot at joining the military. In typical childlike fashion, we imagined the worst. And the worst was damn dramatic. Eventually, I pushed aside my concerns and volunteered for the job. It made me feel like a hero. It scared me to death. Life is a game of "connect the dots" events and decisions. Every dot has the capacity to change the future for better or worse. I was afraid to connect that dot. But I charged ahead anyway. Even then, I was laying the groundwork for what was to come, beginning a pattern that would repeat itself time and time again.

During one of our probes of the roundhouse, Bill had discovered a concrete pad where the workers stacked up wooden crates. We both thought this would make a fine hiding place. It was close to where the mechanics worked and provided excellent cover. It had been a month since we'd inspected the roundhouse interior, so there was a chance the crates had been moved. I told Bill that I would enter and check if the stack of crates was still there. If the hiding place had been compromised, I intended to abort the mission, game over. I further declared that IF they were, and IF I felt comfortable, I would carry out the plan.

The day of the mission dawned at last. We sortied from our base, Bill's house, at midnight and reached the creek an hour later. We were ahead of schedule. As we had done a dozen times before, we crouched there, listened to the rush of the water over polished stones, and studied our objective.

We had constructed a five-point contingency plan to cover a potential mission failure. If I was not back in thirty minutes Bill was to abandon the "Spider's Web" rendezvous point and move to the "Halfway Point." He was to wait there another thirty minutes. If I failed to arrive, he was to assume I had been compromised and captured. At that point he was to return to base and report my loss to the top brass, his parents.

With a heavy heart and a sinking feeling, I embarked. My approach to the roundhouse was a cinch. I knew where all the shadowed spots were and how to move from point A to point B without being seen. Several doors provided entry to the roundhouse. Some were garage doors capable of passing trucks. The one I planned to use was located next to a high-voltage cage that powered the facility. I still remember the buzzing noise the induction motors made and the blue-white glare of electrical spikes dancing all over the transformers.

Stress affects the human mind in odd and sometimes unpredictable ways. There are things I remember clearly about the raid, such as something that smelled like an electrical fire emanating from the high voltage cage and the dark stain of motor oil on the concrete near my boots. But there are things I can't recall, important things, like how or when I entered the building.

I found myself inside the roundhouse, pressed against a wall. I could hear men talking. I could hear electrical tools running. I could hear the chug of a compressor. I smelled grease and sweat.

I took my time. I moved slowly. I controlled my fear. That skill, learned at a young age, would save me more than once on remote battlefields in the future. I moved from point to point, penetrating deeper into the facility. At last I saw the stack of wooden crates that Bill had described. A few of them had been pried open. I could see the contents. The boxes contained train wheels, great steel disks mounted on forged wheels. Their size astounded me. Each one must have weighed a ton. I was standing there in plain sight and wondering how anyone could move such a thing when a guy on a forklift pulled up.

I was so absorbed in studying the wheels that I didn't hear the growling motor of the tractor until it was too late. I froze. I remained motionless while the driver hoisted one of the train wheels then drove off. I remember the tattoo on his muscular bicep. It was green and faded. It was bristling with sails and the colors red, white, and blue. I decided he must have been in the Navy once. I do not remember what he looked like.

He never saw me. I was relieved. I was also ridiculously pleased that my question about the wheels had been answered.

I took a few steps and found a hiding place in and among the boxes. In a matter of ten to fifteen minutes a dozen workers passed by. The visuals were easy. I got good looks at their faces, but I couldn't read their name tags. The tags were on their right breast pockets, and they were passing to the left. I remember feeling annoyed because I was exactly where I needed to be and I still couldn't get the job done.

I felt the time slipping away. I was eager to leave. Just as I made up my mind to bolt, a mechanic approached the stack of crates and lit a cigarette. I could see his name tag clearly. His name was Johnston. Johnston stepped outside to enjoy his smoke. I could see him on the concrete patio outside, blue vapors swirling around his balding head. He was blocking my exit. I had no choice but to wait him out. At last Johnston flicked the butt away and prepared to reenter the roundhouse. Then another mechanic stepped onto the patio and started a conversation with him. They discussed insurance and overtime, subjects that bored me to tears. Johnston lit another cigarette. I fumed. Eventually, finally, they returned to work. I exited the building safely.

Bill had departed the creek. The thirty-minute mark had passed while I was trapped. He was well on his way to the Halfway Point. I got lost in the dark. I panicked. I couldn't find the bridge that I had crossed a hundred times before.

The lessons were piling up. I got through that night and finally made it home. I fell into bed dirty and discouraged. I was beginning to suspect that there was more to the commando way of life than I had imagined.

The constant in all my adventures with Bill was that things never went according to plan, never. We ran practice missions of increasing complexity and scope throughout our high school years. We left the roundhouse behind. It didn't present a challenge anymore. We mounted assaults and raids against condemned buildings in East Pittsburgh near the Westinghouse plant. We climbed up the side of a warehouse using a water drain pipe to the roof and entered the building from the attic. We practiced our newly acquired skills on factories housing hundreds of workers. Not once did a plan go off without a hitch. We screwed up. We encountered constant obstacles. This was my first introduction to Murphy's Law, and it hit me hard.

The failure rate was high. That never changed. It didn't change when I was a kid, and it was no different when I was downrange in Afghanistan and Iraq in later years. If I learned anything from the missions I ran with Bill, it was that obsessive attention to detail is the key to survival.

Bill became a mentor to me. It bothered him that I struggled with many phobias, including a paralyzing terror of heights and water. He made it his mission to assist me in conquering those fears. In time we put them to rest together. He talked me into rappelling off the bridge at the Union Railroad yard in the middle of the night. He took me to the Ohio River, where we swam together. We swam in the shallows at first, then we headed for deep water. He was always by my side. My fears faded. Soon I was swimming on my own and nothing could strike fear in my heart. I embraced the horrors that haunted me and overcame the fears associated with them. This takes time, but with the proper motivation it's 100 percent achievable. In thinking back on my phobia, I recall that it wasn't about being in deep water at all. What bothered me was that I couldn't see the bottom. It was very odd, and I've never made sense of it.

How do you thank a person for giving you the gift of confidence? You thank them by living a life worthy of their friendship. You live a life of strength and honor, integrity and moral fortitude. I honored Bill by serving my country and taking the fight to those who threatened our way of life. I became a human version of the Sword of Damocles, vanquishing those who chose to test my courage and who threatened the ones I loved. For me, war and combat are personal. Anyone who tells you different, that it's just business, has never served in a special operations unit. End of story.

As fate would have it, Bill passed away in a bizarre accident as a young adult. Life is surprising. Just when you think you have it nailed down, the screw turns and you find yourself living in a completely different world. I dodged bullets in Afghanistan and Iraq. I placed my neck on the line hundreds of times and only suffered minor scratches.

Bill got out of his car one sunny day, tripped on the curb, and cracked his head open on the sidewalk. He got up and walked away from the injury. But an aneurysm caused by the blow to his skull struck him down a short time later.

My father called me and gave me the news. He wasn't one to make phone calls. He had a difficult time expressing emotion. The failure of his marriage and the death of the only woman he loved had dented him badly. I accepted his failures. I understood him. I loved him without reservation.

He asked if I had heard about Bill's death. I'd spoken to my old friend on the phone just a month before. I argued with my father. I tried to convince him that he had the wrong Bill. Then he picked up the paper and read the obituary to me. There was no mistaking Bill's resume and history.

As fate would have it, Bill had joined the Navy in hopes of becoming a SEAL, but color blindness had disqualified him from the opportunity. He was a radio operator for the four years he did serve. Ironically, his older brother, Jim, was a member of SEAL Team 2. One summer day I was at Bill's house when Jim walked into the room. Immediately I noticed his long beard and hair. I said to him, "Hey, Jim, how long you been out of the Navy?" His response shocked me. "I'm still in, just on a new team." Little did I know that he was one of the original members—a "plank owner"—of the Navy's elite counterterrorist unit, SEAL Team 6, a unit that I would work with closely while serving in Afghanistan in the latter years of my special operations career.

But this day, while on the phone with my father, the news of Bill's death stunned me. It took a while for the information to sink in. Then I phoned Bill's parents. I had called him so many times I still knew the phone number. I spoke to his mother. She confirmed that he had died. As always, she showed me kindness. She was strong. She was a woman of deep faith. She explained that Bill's death was God's will and that he was in a better place. She proceeded to ask how I had been getting on. She wanted to know what I was doing with my life, whether I was married, where I was living, etc., etc. Like Bill, she was a natural mentor. She guided me through the first waves of grief. She distracted me with talk of friends and family. I held back the tears that I knew would flow the second I hung up the phone. That talk made me stronger.

Bill wasn't the last friend I lost. Many more would follow. Some succumbed to disease and violent accidents. Some died in combat, and I held their hands while they passed. The years and life rolled on. I found myself under fire in Afghanistan and Iraq. During these times of high stress, when my adrenaline was pumping and I was deeply afraid, I flashed back to my roundhouse adventures with Bill. Our dreams had become reality. I was a commando at last. But Bill wasn't around to share in my adventures.

Bill was gone.

My childhood was gone.

Death was all around me.

There would be no more wooden guns.

7

OUT OF SCHOOL

"Americans love to fight. All real Americans
love the sting of battle."

—GEORGE S. PATTON

AND INTO THE FIRE

I ENTERED THE SERVICE immediately after high school. Ten
days after graduation I was doing push-ups to the hoarse music of a
Marine drill instructor's (DI's) insults. I was running miles daily in
the sweltering summer heat on South Carolina's Parris Island. The
Marines wasted no time in shaping up and breaking down recruit
candidates. It all started at 0500 in the morning.

I was placed on a bus for the drive to the Island at the MEPs
station in Pittsburgh. We rolled through the gates hours before
dawn. That was when the first terrifying lesson was delivered. I had
been dozing. I wouldn't be allowed to do that again for weeks to
come. The bus came to a halt with a clashing of gears, the lights
snapped on, and a burly drill instructor clambered aboard. He took

one look at the frightened passengers, called us "fucking worms," then roared out a series of confusing commands. When we didn't react appropriately and immediately, he got angry. He got spitting mad. He said, "I'm done being nice!"

I thought, *I guess all that yelling beforehand was him being nice.* I didn't say it of course. I knew better than to say a thing in that environment. Even then, I was a survivor.

The DI called upon his DI buddies then. They invaded the bus in camouflage uniforms so neatly pressed that they looked ready for a general's inspection. They were muscular and mean. They ripped people from their seats, tore off their backpacks, and sent them stumbling through the doors to the concrete pad outside. The welcome wasn't any warmer out there. We were kicked and shoved into rough lines and ranks. Chaos reigned.

It was apparent to me from the first minute that the instructors were hell-bent on weeding out the "nonhackers" from the get-go, those not worthy enough to serve in their beloved Corps. There were a lot of fearful tears, but none from me.

Some guys complained that they wanted to go home, which I found astonishing. The long bus ride had given them too much time to think about what was to come. And when the yelling started, it was too much for them to handle. I couldn't imagine what had possessed them to try to join the Marines in the first place.

On the other hand, I was excited. I had waited for this moment for years, and it was upon me at last. I would find out once and for all what I was made of. I'd been told all my life that I would never cut it as a Marine, let alone anything else. I'd heard it all, that I was too skinny, I was too graceless, and I had no athletic ability . . . blah, blah, blah. My confidence in my physical ability up to this point was nonexistent. I knew I had a long road to hoe.

I wasn't on the island twenty-four hours before I was stripped of everything, including my hair. I remember the barbershop and the piles and piles of blond, red, and brown fuzz on the green tile floor and the screams of drill instructors for us to stand at attention while each of us got fleeced.

I don't know what Marine Corps boot camp is like now, but back in the early '80s it was not a "more understanding and caring" service. Things were different for sure. That first twenty-four hours was a shock to the system. We endured urinalysis together. We trudged through equipment issue. I was given a uniform two sizes too large by a supply clerk who didn't have one that fit me. Even our covers (hats) didn't fit me correctly. We got punished because some people couldn't pee under pressure. We got yelled at for stepping off the painted lines that were supposed to guide us from place to place. We got drilled for looking at one another or glancing at the sky and wishing we were on a plane to someplace, anyplace but Parris Island.

We fell out on the grinder in ranks after the haircuts. We were already getting the hang of lining up and standing still. The various positions we were supposed to assume, like attention and at ease, would be taught to us later. I stole a glance at my fellow sufferers. All of us were bald, and a few scalps were bleeding from the brutal shaving. We were jug-eared and indistinguishable from one another. We looked like a bunch of department store dummies without wigs. I didn't recognize a single face.

I remember falling into my assigned bunk at some point. I didn't know what time it was. I had lost all track of the hours after they took my watch. I was so exhausted that I didn't care whether it was day or night. I just wanted to close my eyes and drift away. A small voice in my head kept moaning, "You asked for it. You got it."

They gave us about fifteen minutes to fall asleep. Then they came in screaming. My second full day in Marine Corps boot camp was underway.

Boot camp was tough. For those who weren't committed, it was impossible. They fell away quickly. Two or three a week failed to meet the standards or quit on their own. They were hauled off for de-processing. The daily physical and mental grind was designed to destroy any rebellion, to exhaust you to the point that you would follow orders without thinking. Later we would be taught that thinking was vitally important, that a US Marine's ability to focus and make independent decisions under stress was vitally important. This was my first glimpse at what was to follow over the years in regards to performing under pressure.

Life was a steady drumbeat. We rose early, usually well before dawn. We were herded outside to a massive asphalt parade deck for PT (physical training). We ran, did push-ups, sit-ups, and a plethora of other torturous physical drills for a few hours. Then we were given minutes to assemble our uniforms and dress ourselves. We marched, in step, to the chow hall. Then some other activity was in store, whether it involved a mass inspection, close order drill, an introduction to our rifles, or even class time. I was surprised at how demanding the academics were. Learning the military Code of Conduct was only the beginning. We studied the history of the Corps, to include its inception and greatest battles. We learned tradition. We were expected to recite the General Orders verbatim. For some reason, reciting the General Orders during an inspection always gave me trouble. I'm not sure why. All of this information and more was written in a large binder about as thick as a dictionary they called "The Big Red Monster."

I enjoyed Sundays. We were allowed to attend church services if we wanted. When I heard you could sneak a few minutes of sleep while services were going on, I signed up. I didn't have any desire to break the rules. I was just exhausted, and I wanted every advantage I could gain to fight through the long days, perform at my maximum, and keep my head screwed on straight.

As the days passed I found my groove and my confidence began to build. I had been prepping for challenges of boot camp and the Corps all my life. I had studied what basic training entailed. I had spoken to Marines in high school who related their experiences to me and told me what to expect. Most of the people around me hadn't done anything at all to prepare. The head games caught them by surprise.

They didn't understand why they were being tested or what the end-game might be. Some adapted. Some didn't. I soared like an eagle. I actually began to enjoy it.

I stayed focused. I kept my head down. It's never smart to draw unnecessary attention to yourself. My senior drill instructor had his favorites. But being his favorite wasn't a good thing. It meant you could be rattled and then he could punish you over and over. My DI often said, "No one is a total loss. You can always serve as a bad example for the rest of humanity." He meant it. He was more than happy to dish out pain for a brain fart. In those days the DI's could lay their hands on you. They often did. I never saw anyone get hit, but there was plenty of rough handling.

I worked hard and tried to be invisible. As it turns out, I wasn't invisible at all. The instructors had noticed me plenty. And they liked what they saw.

I was at the front of the class in more than a few respects. Rarely did I "spotlight" myself and cause the DI's to punish me. They were constantly looking for a reason to jump on someone for doing something stupid. It was a daily thing, right up to graduation. My physical ability was improving weekly, and I knew it. So was my confidence.

Eventually, I came face to face with the legendary "O-Course." This was a massive obstacle course designed by the Marine Corps to separate the wheat from the chaff and the weak from the strong. I had seen photos of this thing in magazines and books while I was in high school and couldn't wait to give it a try. To my absolute amazement, I took to the course like I had been training for it my whole life. Many of the recruits were in far better physical shape than me, but they couldn't beat the obstacles. The ropes, logs, and structures you had to climb over were just too much for them to manage. Their weight and poor upper body strength were their undoing. Worse, some of them were just plain terrified.

One obstacle in particular seemed to unnerve lots of the recruits. The thing looked like a giant ladder made out of logs. It was probably forty- to fifty-feet high. You didn't want to fall from that height. If it didn't kill you, the landing would sure cause some serious injuries.

I actually looked forward to hitting the O-Course! Most of the guys hated it. I didn't understand why. Once again the drill instructors were watching and noted my motivation level and enthusiastic performance. I even remember hearing a few of them compliment me under their breath when they thought nobody was listening. In one instance one of my DI's actually said, "Good job, Teti." They rarely did that. These motivational breadcrumbs fueled my furnace. I wanted more.

In boot camp, we were given a week of swim training. This isn't floaties and paddling lessons, folks. We were instructed in the basics of water survival. We were dressed in full uniforms, outfitted with packs, and flung into the deep end of a pool. I admit, I was not a strong swimmer. My confidence was not where it needed to be. The pool was very different from the O-Course, which I had excelled at. I approached this newest obstacle with dread.

Once again some strange inner strength hit me like a runaway train. It wasn't easy, but I slogged through pool week and emerged victorious. We did all sorts of drills in the pool to build confidence and learn basic water survival skills. I was taught how to turn my pants into a flotation device. One drill required half the class to get into the deep end of the pool and tread water. While there, we were handed what the instructors called a "physical training brick." It was a rubber-covered block of something or other that weighed a hefty ten pounds. We were ordered to keep the thing dry. We were told to tread water while holding the brick over our heads. It sounds easy enough, but try it wearing heavy combat boots and a full uniform. It was a nightmare. I'm pretty sure I swallowed a gallon of pool water before I got the hang of it.

There was a lot vomiting going on during the exercises. There was vomit in the water and on the tiles surrounding the pool. The water challenges had a devastating effect on many of my fellow recruits. They weren't prepared, and they ingested way too much water.

I suffered through every day of pool week. I hated it, but I hung in there and kept paddling until it was over. I would go on to a Spec Ops career that required the development of very advanced water survival and swimming skills, far beyond even what most strong swimmers would call normal. At the time I had no idea how many hours of my life would be used up swimming in the freezing Chesapeake Bay or in chlorine pools. I am amazed at many phobias I beat back and the number of weaknesses I overcame in order to succeed. But in a way, I'm not surprised. I was a highly motivated person. I'd had so many bad breaks growing up, I'd lost count. Everyone has them, but how you react to them determines who you are as an adult and how you'll tackle life's O-Course. If you give up and turn inward, you'll fail at just about everything. On the other hand, if you react positively and become determined to win, no matter the odds or obstacles, you *will* succeed. My mother told me over and over that I could do anything I wanted if I wanted it badly enough. She was right of course.

Toward the end of boot camp we spent two weeks at the rifle range. I was beyond excited to be there. I had waited a long time to fire a real M16.

We loaded up all our gear and marched through blistering heat to a barracks located alongside the firing range. We moved in. We would live there for the duration of our basic marksmanship training.

The next day we were on the range "snapping-in."

I wasn't prepared in any way for what came next. I'd had no real experience with weapons. In time I would come to appreciate how the Marine Corps taught shooting to its recruits. No other service does it like the Corps. Still, I didn't enjoy a minute of the experience.

Snapping-in consisted of five days of learning the shooting positions: standing, sitting, kneeling, and being prone. We were divided into groups of ten to twelve recruits. We sat around fifty-five-gallon drums with small targets painted on them. We spent agonizing hours locked into the firing positions. I found the crouching, lying, and standing to be very painful over time. The agony was compounded by a canvas weapon sling tightened to my nonfiring arm like a tourniquet.

We didn't fire a round for five long days. We sat for hours in the baking sun, with sweat dripping down our backs, trying hard not to flick away the sand fleas that landed on our faces and crawled into our ears. It sucked, but I learned the positions.

The range distinguished the men from the boys. In every class, a few exhibited excellent marksmanship skills. I surprised myself. I was one of two standouts in my company. I went head-to-head with a polite Southerner. I believe he was an Alabamian, about as redneck as they come. We fought it out for top honors, but a long history of squirrel and coon hunting with his daddy's old Remington gave him an edge. My wooden commando rifle hadn't contributed much to my proficiency. I heard that my rival went on to become an accomplished sniper and was the honor graduate of the prestigious Scout Sniper Course. I did not mind being beaten in that instance. He was an excellent shot, and I envied his skill.

Those two weeks at the rifle range were a surprise and a joy. The desire to join Spec Ops became firmly cemented in my mind. I felt oddly comfortable around the noise and regimented chaos of a shooting range. From the get-go, holding a rifle seemed natural to me. It was a tool as instantly familiar and usable as a pencil or spoon. I was in my element and didn't yet understand why. Once again, my success at something unexpected boosted my confidence.

My abilities had progressed to the point that the instructors decided to reward me for my performance. They had seen something in it that they found impressive. Come graduation day, I was meritoriously promoted to private first class (PFC).

My father was watching from the stands. He was deeply proud of me. My only regret was that my mother was not there to see what I had accomplished. There are no words I can find to describe the sense of loss I felt that day. Her death hit me again like a sledgehammer, and I unsuccessfully fought the tears when I was being promoted to PFC. I was elated at my graduation and the honors heaped on me, but I was deeply saddened that she was not there to share in my victory. The mix of emotions was indescribable. I cried with pride, happiness, and terrible sadness all at once.

I had fought through the long and brutal weeks of training and emerged a US Marine. It was an incomparable feeling. I had put behind me the naysayers who questioned my strength, passion, and dedication to a cause. Though it seems like a much smaller accomplishment in my rearview mirror, it remains and always will be one of the proudest moments of my life. I have had many positions and jobs and have fought on distant battlefields wearing different uniforms, but I am and will always be a US Marine.

Following boot camp, I headed for Infantry Training School (ITS) at Camp Geiger, North Carolina. I had read all about ITS. I'd imagined being there many times. At last I'd made it. I was born to be a warrior. I belonged there.

I flourished. I sailed through the training. I passed each test that was thrown at me. Nothing caught me off guard. It all felt so effortless and easy. Those days are a seamless blur in my memory now. I wasn't really working hard. But again, I was recognized for my performance. I was awarded Distinguished Honor Graduate and meritoriously promoted to lance corporal (LCPL). Being promoted meritoriously in the Marines is not an easy feat. Doing it twice in training is almost unheard of.

After the ITS graduation ceremony, we were instructed to fall out in the barracks. When we arrived, I saw three men waiting in the center of the room. They had Marine Corps gold jump wings and scuba diver "bubbles" pinned to their uniforms. In an instant I knew they were from the Corps' legendary 2nd Force Recon Company. These guys were revered as the "elite of the elite" in the Marines. Affectionately referred to as the "Company," they were the USMC's most dangerous and accomplished warriors. At the time they were the Corps' only command with Spec Ops qualifications and aspirations. What I didn't know was that they were bastard children. They were not officially recognized as a special operations group and weren't a component of SOCOM (Special Operations Command). As a result, they were chronically underfunded. They weren't given proper gear, nor were they utilized in real world operations.

At the time I was ignorant of all that. The three men explained that they were looking for new meat to try out for the Company.

One of them asked, "Who's the honor grad here? Stand up!"

I stood up and responded sharply, "I am, sir!"

He laughed out loud. Then he asked, "You think you have what it takes to join our ranks?"

I didn't like his dismissive attitude. It made me mad. So I snapped, "There's only one way to find out. Where do I sign, sir?"

Then he addressed me in a bone-chilling, extraordinarily calm voice. I had never heard such an unforgiving tone all laced up with pleasure before. It bordered on crazy. But I would hear it again, later and often. Men who were about to kill someone in cold blood used that voice. He growled, "I can guarantee you will regret saying that."

His words scared the hell out of me, but I wasn't about to back down. I knew without a doubt that I wanted to stand shoulder-to-shoulder with the best of the best; 2nd Force Recon was the toughest fighting unit the Marine Corps had ever fielded. I made it my mission then and there to join their ranks and prove him wrong.

The next day I reported to 2nd Force Reconnaissance Company in French Creek, Camp Lejeune, North Carolina. I strolled down the hallway of Company headquarters in full dress uniform, carrying my service and medical records. I knocked on the first sergeant's hatch and introduced myself.

The man who greeted me was well over six feet tall and weighed 250 pounds or more. He had a bull neck, corded muscles, and forearms like Popeye. I thought he looked like some kind of superhero. They should have used him to decorate Marine Corps recruiting posters. But now that I think about it, that wouldn't have worked. You need a sympathetic face for those posters. He was completely devoid of emotion. He had a bullet-shaped head. He had no mercy in his eyes. He looked at me dismissively, like I was a pizza delivery boy.

Without a word, he returned to his office. Through the open door, I saw him searching for something in his desk. Shortly he returned with a piece of chalk. He bent and drew a small circle on the deck. It was about the size of a softball. Then he straightened to his full height and glowered at me. He barked, "Fill the circle with sweat!"

I had no idea what to do. I stood there in the brightly lit corridor and looked up at him quizzically. I didn't like where things were going. I felt like an idiot. And my ignorance was just making him angry.

He knocked the records from my hand and screamed at me to get in push-up position. He yelled in my ear, "Marine, I said fill the circle with sweat!"

I dropped, placed my palms on the deck, and balanced on the tips of my toes. I was good at push-ups. I lost track of how many of them I did in that hallway and how many Marines stepped over my smartly dressed form and kept on walking. None of them gave me a second look or seemed to care. I could have been a dead body lying there, and nobody would have paid me any mind. It was bewildering.

The trick, I learned, was to let the sweat dribble down my nose and drip into the circle. It took a long time. But eventually, I filled the chalk circle with my sweat.

I yelled out, "First Sergeant, the circle is filled!"

He stomped out of his office with a five-foot length of thick iron chain clutched in his hands. I wondered what the hell he was going to do with it. The heavy links could have anchored the Queen Mary.

He made me stand at attention. My dress blues were soaked with perspiration, and I was deeply unhappy. He handed me the chain and said, "From now on, when I see you, you'd better be carrying this chain. You sleep with it. You shit with it. You march with it. You shoot with it. You jerk off with it. But I better not see you jerking off. Do you understand me, Lance Corporal Teti?"

I replied meekly, "Yes, sir."

He pretended he couldn't hear me. He snapped, "What? What the fuck did you say, Lance Corporal Teti?" My rank and name were beginning to sound like some kind of curse.

I shouted, "YES, SIR!"

For the next eight weeks I was physically beaten down. It happened every day, all day. The RIP or Recon Indoctrination Platoon, had their way with little Lance Corporal Teti. Their purpose was simple and evil: They were tasked with making me quit. They wanted me to abandon any ambition to join 2nd Force. I fought back hard. I was angry. I was hell-bent on beating them at their own game. It's always been that way with me. No one tells me I can't do something I want to do.

I got very little sleep during those eight weeks. A lot of that time is a blur. One stint of sleep deprivation lasted three long days. All I remember was being cold, wet, sick to my stomach and nursing a half-dozen blisters on my feet. I gradually realized I wasn't the only one in that nightmare. There were other "candidates." We spent hours daily in a pool and in French Creek. The water was freezing cold. When we weren't working out or running obstacle courses, we were soaking in the icy waters of French Creek. I was wet 50 percent of the time. Now and then I was allowed to dry out. I was grateful when that happened, but it never lasted long. They were toughening us up and trying to determine our breaking points. This period of torture turned out to be a mere warm-up for the next challenge. Amphibious Reconnaissance School (ARS) was the second step in the grueling list of requirements necessary to earn my Reconnaissance Marine rating (0321) and join the 2nd.

I attended ARS in the winter. At the time the school was located at Fort Story, Virginia. It was bitterly cold when I arrived. I can still remember how spartan the compound was. The entire installation consisted of several old-school Quonset huts and a small classroom building. The muddy half-acre was surrounded by a twelve-foot high razor-wire fence. I've never been so cold. The showers offered no hot water. I'm not kidding. I didn't warm up the entire time I was there.

The course lasted nine weeks. It was brutal as a rule, but the winter conditions made it a real gut check. We performed day and night swims in the freezing Chesapeake Bay. We went on long beach runs with and without rucksacks. We ground out hundreds of push-ups and sit-ups daily. This was supposed to provide us with a basic foundation of reconnaissance skills. It was mind numbing.

The course stressed highly disciplined camouflage skills during the patrol phase. I hated it. The oil-based camo paint made my face break out. I got the worst case of acne I've ever had. I've still got some scars.

The odds of graduating were poor. I saw strong men fall by the wayside with torn muscles, broken bones, tendonitis, hypothermia, infections from blisters, and terrible back injuries that would likely plague them all their lives. Courses like ARS, BUD/S, and Ranger School are specifically designed to break a man down slowly, mentally and physically. The exercises are a deliberately engineered continuous grind that will beat down even the most physically fit human beings.

Mental toughness is a necessity. In some ways it is more important than how much muscle a candidate possesses. Without the motivation to endure, there is no possible chance that an individual can succeed. Out of a starting class of forty-five men, twelve managed to stay the course and graduate ARS. I was one of them. Eventually, finally, I came aboard 2nd Force Recon.

I spent three years with the Company. At the time we were between wars and the US military wasn't engaged in any regional conflicts. I never deployed on a combat mission. I spent day after day, week after week, and year after year in training. The call to action never came. It was frustrating to say the least.

I spent my last year of service stationed in Okinawa, Japan. I was working with 3rd Recon Battalion. I trained with the Republic of Korea (ROK) Marines, with Thailand's SEAL teams, and Philippine Special Ops. Although I never went to war as a Marine, it laid a solid foundation for what was to come. Eventually, in succeeding years, I would join one of the most secretive government counterterrorist units in the world. I would fight far from home. I would cheat death again and again.

Four years passed. So much had happened that I could barely recall the day I rolled into Parris Island and was yanked off that bus. I had come far, suffered much, and tested myself under the harshest conditions imaginable. And my enlistment was finally up. I thought hard about my future. I wasn't unhappy with my tour as a Recon Marine, but I was displeased with the Corps' dismissive treatment of its lone Spec Ops group. The brass had no love for the Company. We all felt like redheaded stepchildren. I had had enough. I decided to take my chances as a civilian.

No one questioned my level of motivation and commitment to the Corps. I achieved everything possible in that four-year time frame and kept myself ready to fight. But my timing was completely off. I landed between wars and attached myself to a unit that wasn't properly supported. In February 2006 the Corps officially established Marine Special Operations Command (MARSOC). At last the Marine Recon groups had a home, equipment, and a mission. They would go on to spearhead some of the toughest fights in the history of the Marine Corps. But I wouldn't be with them.

8

THE TAO OF CAPITALISM

"In the business world, the rearview mirror is always clearer than the windshield."

—WARREN BUFFET

OR HOW TO FAIL AT BUSINESS WITHOUT REALLY TRYING

I'M GOAL-DRIVEN. I'VE been that way since I was very young. As I mentioned previously, I had been focused like a laser on one thing during my youth, joining the Marine Corps. When that part of my life was over, I felt adrift. I didn't know what to do or where to go. I was twenty-one years old and had no prospects or a plan. It was frightening. But it was exhilarating too. It's a relief to purge an overbearing authoritarian structure like the Marine Corps from your life. You can breathe again. But at the same time, it leaves you craving structure and a mission.

After my time in the Corps ended, I rented a hotel room, got to work studying my options, and began making phone calls to contacts I had maintained over the years. I didn't have hard skills that would make me valuable to a company. I didn't consider sales. I had seen my father try and fail miserably at that difficult craft, so I had no desire to try it.

I admire good salespeople. They are among the toughest-minded men and women I know. They are fast-talking artists in a profession that seems easy on the surface but involves some of the hardest, most dehumanizing and underappreciated work on the planet. I will tell you something about capitalism that most people don't get, a life lesson that my father taught me: On a level, we are all salespeople. It's critical to understand that every single job and most human interactions involve some sort of sales skill. If you're not selling a product directly, you're selling yourself or your work. It's just that simple.

I didn't really understand it at the time, but the Marines had given me a whole toolbox of skills that would prove crucial in the years of struggle and capitalist endeavors to come. I had a work ethic right out of the box, but the Corps had hammered it home. By the time they finished with me, discipline and physical labor were such a part of who I was that I couldn't imagine taking time off for myself. I still can't, which is why I rise early, work out hard, shower up, and then, and only then, begin my day. I literally do more before 0900 than most people do all day.

By the time I got to bed that first night out of the Corps, I had a plan in place and a temporary residence lined up. I was headed for Las Vegas. My cousin Jack had extended an invitation to "come visit and unwind for a while." I felt it was a fitting time to do so. I had never been to Sin City, but the descriptions of the place intrigued me. Hell, I was twenty-one and ready to have a good time!

I stepped off a bus to blistering desert heat in the summer of 1986. Jack had a ranch house located about four miles off the strip.

I walked there because I had limited funds and didn't want to waste a dime. At the time my attitude was, "Why pay to ride when I've got two perfectly good walking sticks?"

Jack was a well-known percussionist who had attended some of the most prestigious music schools in the country. He could play pretty much any musical device that required beating, tapping, or shaking, from the drums to the timpani to the xylophone to the spoons, with equal ease. His basement walls were lined with mementos and instruments that he had collected over the years. He had played for Sammy Davis Jr., Wayne Newton, and other top stars in Vegas. He was at the top of the food chain in his industry.

Despite Jack's renown and a nonstop train of gigs that earned him big bucks, he was disciplined. He could have played any one of those instruments blindfolded, and occasionally he did, but he didn't take a day off. He practiced every day, seven days a week. It was amazing to watch him at work. Living with the man convinced me that discipline was the key to any success. His work ethic had a lifelong impact on me. I still reflect on it and act accordingly to this day.

I arrived in Vegas with about $4,000 in the bank. This comprised my entire life savings. It was all I had to show for four years of back-breaking work in the Marine Corps. The money didn't last of course. Before I knew it, I was down to my last few hundred dollars. I decided the blackjack tables weren't going to provide me with a living. Vacation was over. I needed to find a job.

A few weeks after I arrived in Vegas, I met a girl who changed my life. We fell into a push-me-pull-me-on-again-off-again relationship that lasted for five long years. If you'd told me it was going to happen beforehand, I would have laughed in your face. I would have told you the odds of beating the house in Vegas were a whole lot better than any chance I would fall for a woman hard. I had no idea anyone could shake my world the way she did. Life can and *will* take you down strange roads. A word of caution here: Some of those roads may be mined.

The woman who turned my head was highly educated and whip-smart. Tina was her name. She had earned a master's degree in economics from Princeton. She was stunningly beautiful, driven, competitive, and witty. She had carved out a place for herself in a man's world long before she fell into my life like a live hand grenade. She was a successful stockbroker at Bear Stearns. She was one of the best brokers in the Vegas office at the time.

We had a natural rapport. We talked about everything. We closed down restaurants because we couldn't stop jabbering and completely forgot to eat. It was the most natural and easygoing relationship I had ever had. One night at dinner, Tina dropped a bomb on me. She said, "You know what? You've got the gift of gab. People like you make perfect stockbrokers. You ever think about going for your licenses and doing what I do?"

I had never considered it. I had imagined, wrongly, that a college degree was required to buy and sell stocks and bonds. I was young and had plenty of opinions that were incorrect. The brainy woman across the table explained that to me in an amused voice. She told me that I only needed to be licensed, which sounded easy enough. I was wrong about that too.

My lack of education didn't disqualify me, but acquiring the licenses was beyond my means. I had about $150 in the bank. I didn't have a pot to piss in or a window to throw it out of. I needed to pass several courses, specifically the Longman Series at the University of Nevada, Las Vegas, to meet the criteria for taking the Series 7 and Series 63 broker exams. The tuition alone was $1,500. Worse, the failure rate for first-time test takers was 90 percent. The house odds definitely weren't in my favor.

When I admitted how dire my finances were, Tina volunteered the money. She said,

"I guarantee you, with my tutoring you'll crush the tests and you'll make money as a broker. Then you'll pay me back with interest. Deal?" She said the Longman Series at UNLV was dry as dust and deadly boring. She thought of all sorts of ways to spice up the learning process. We studied four days a week for several hours a night at her place. I remember to this day one of the books was thick as an old-school phone book.

I was staggered by the amount of information a would-be stockbroker needed to master to earn his or her qualifications. I began the Longman Series in the summer of 1987. Most of the students in my class had advanced degrees in economics, business, and accounting. And Tina wasn't kidding. The classes were brutal. I faced down a never-ending stream of mind-numbing topics, including, among others, security industry and law, IPO structure and valuations, evaluation methods of PE ratios, the exercise of warrants, REITS, mutual fund management and administration, and last but certainly not least, trading options. Worse, there was math involved. Even worse, the classes were held in a room with a failing air conditioner. After my long study sessions with Tina, I arrived at school exhausted. The heat and dry-as-chalk subject matter made it nearly impossible to stay awake. I actually stood through most of my classes. Surviving the training was a huge test of my willpower and determination.

Life went on outside the classroom. Tina and I fell apart and fell together again. On May 4, 1988 the UNLV campus was rocked by a massive concussive shockwave radiating from a distant, massive explosion. The drop ceiling in the hot classroom collapsed and landed on our heads. I was uninjured, but several students were transported to the hospital with scalp and facial lacerations. More were injured in the mass panic that followed.

I headed out to a balcony to try to assess the cause of the detonation. I saw hundreds of students running for their lives. I was convinced that some sort of an attack had occurred. I hadn't been out of the military long enough to forget that the world was a dangerous place. I guessed that a terrorist bomb had gone off at the Edward W. Clark Generating Station, which was off to the west. But then I saw smoke to the east, in the direction of Henderson. As I stood there wondering what could possibly interest a terrorist in Henderson, I felt the rumble and roll of a second, more powerful explosion. I saw a momentary incendiary flash. In the seconds following I observed a boiling mushroom cloud rising over the desert town. This latest blast rocked the foundation of the building I was standing atop and convinced me that I should get to the ground level. I was convinced that a nuke had been detonated to the west and we were all in a lot of trouble.

As it turned out, I was wrong but not by much. A plant belonging to the Pacific Engineering and Production Company of Nevada, or PEPCON, was located in Henderson. PEPCON was one of two American producers of ammonium perchlorate, an oxidizer used in solid propellant rocket boosters. The US Air Force and the Space Shuttle program were the principal purchasers of the chemical. As I later learned, a fire broke out at the plant and quickly spread to holding tanks containing the volatile oxidizer. The damage from the ensuing blast leveled the plant and damaged homes and businesses up to five miles away. There were shattered windows, injuries from the flying glass and debris, doors blown off hinges, and cars and trucks overturned on the nearby highway. A 737 on approach to McCarran International Airport was buffeted by the second shockwave, but the pilot stayed steady and managed to avert a costlier human disaster.

There were hundreds of injuries but only two deaths. Fortunately, the plant was mostly empty at the time of the so-called PEPCON disaster. In a later study, investigators concluded that the largest explosion was equivalent to the detonation of a kiloton of TNT, which is roughly the yield of a small nuclear weapon.

Eventually, finally, I completed my coursework and felt ready to take a swipe at the Series 7 and 63 exams. I doubted I would pass. Hardly anyone did, and I was a relentlessly average student. I was as ready as I would ever be. I had extra incentive. I'd applied to Bear Stearns for a position and was accepted provisionally, with the caveat that I pass my exams on the first try. Additionally, they offered to pay my full tuition if I met that high bar and came aboard.

The Series 7, at that time, consisted of 250 multiple choice questions. I had six hours to complete the test. This involved plenty of math, and I was expected to show my notes and methodology. The only thing I was permitted to bring into the testing room was a handful of No. 2 pencils and the clothes on my back. Notes, books, and calculators were banned.

I sat down at my desk and said to myself, "You can do this. To hell with all these people and their master's degrees."

I took the full six hours, pacing myself carefully. I'd been told that the test was almost as hard as the bar exam. I don't have any experience in law, but I can tell you the exam was ridiculously difficult. With just over one minute to answer each question, there was little time to think things through. You knew the answer or you didn't. There was no gray area or time for waffling. A minimal score of 75 percent was required to pass. Failing meant I would be barred from retesting for thirty days and I'd be forced to cough up the fees all over again. A different test was offered each time so that no one could compromise the exam, which meant things wouldn't get any easier. It also meant I would be on the hook for the full tuition amount and the position at Bear Stearns wouldn't be available. There was a lot on the line in that room. I don't mind saying that I was scared. When I turned in my exam and left the room, I was bathed in sweat.

A week later I received a call from the office manager at Bear Stearns. She said, "Mr. Teti, I received your test results from UNLV, and I wanted to give you an update. We do this as a courtesy for all prospective hires."

Her tone wasn't encouraging. Her words were brisk and dry. My heart sank. I said, "Go ahead. I can take it. Give it to me straight, ma'am."

She didn't laugh. After a long moment, she replied, "You passed. Welcome aboard Bear Stearns, Mr. Teti."

I was thunderstruck. I actually argued with her. I blurted, "No way. There's no way I passed. You sure about that?" The little voice in my skull screamed, *What the hell are you doing? Shut up, you moron!* I closed my trap at once.

Finally, she laughed. She said, "No mistake. You're our newest hire, Mr. Teti. None of the other candidates passed the Series 7 and 63. Congratulations!"

I sighed with relief. I could barely believe it. The long study sessions with Tina at her place hadn't resulted in a lot of actual studying. I had sleepwalked through the classes. But somehow, I'd absorbed the necessary information and passed the test. I learned later that most of my fellow candidates took it three or more times before passing. It was a victory worth savoring.

I remained at Bear Stearns for five years. I went to work every day dressed in a suit and tie and arrived on time. I took lunch at my desk. I worked late hours. I learned everything I could about the market and sales. Selling was crucial to trading, which came as a surprise to me. The ability to sell was absolutely paramount, and I honed my pitch to a fine art. I finally understood why my father had struggled for so many years at the craft and failed again and again. He was missing a key ingredient: talent. There is no middle ground in sales. You have the talent to sell, or you don't. You're a great salesman, or you're a lousy salesman. I know that sounds rude and cruel, but those are the painful facts. If you're a lousy salesman, you aren't going to get better. Get out of the game. It's like trying to polish a turd. You just can't.

The job was difficult to say the least. In those days automated dialers and cellular technology weren't around. We hand-dialed the phones. We weren't permitted to head home until we'd made 400 calls. As well as being very wise, my branch manager was a slave master. He'd sit at his desk in front of the "bullpen" and yell out little encouragements like, "Don't pick up that bag, Mr. Smith. You've got fifteen calls to make before you can see your wife and kids." Sometimes he threatened us. Sometimes he supported us. And now and then he offered the rare reward. He knew what he was doing. He knew how to manage people and money. But most of all, he knew how to sell. He could sell a ketchup popsicle to a lady wearing white gloves in the middle of July. He imparted a lot of wisdom to me over those five years. I absorbed everything he told me. The training and experience I received at Bear Stearns would prove useful over and over in my life. I learned how to make and grow money, how to manage it, how to invest it, and when to let go of a failing project. And finally, I learned to appreciate how hard it is to really make money. I also understood the age-old adage that goes, "A fool and his money are soon parted."

The tools I took from that job have resulted in a steady flow of cash into my coffers over the years despite the ups and downs in my life. At the end of my Bear Stearns period, there were more downs than ups. Tina and I parted permanently. I grew lonely. I tried to fill the void with work. I reveled in the strict routine and discipline meted out by my branch manager. I stayed at my desk like an anchor. I remained when everyone else grew exhausted, left, and quit. The turnover in trading was and is exceedingly high. The long hours and grueling monthly requirements set for the brokers is self-defeating. Eventually, finally, everyone breaks. I saw better men turn to alcohol and drugs, completely destroying their lives. The stress of maintaining a desk and making their monthly quotas was more than most could handle.

Eventually, finally, I broke too. As I mentioned, I had learned plenty about building wealth. One of the things you hear most often is that you need to be in the right place at the right time to invest successfully. I'll add to that. Not only do you need to be in the right place at the right time, you need to be in the right market, with the right amount of money, with the right people.

I could say a lot more about that in excruciating detail, but instead I'll let my life make the point. The mistake I committed next, after leaving Bear Stearns, perfectly illustrates the theme and the title of this chapter.

Everyone has considered starting their own business. Few do. Fewer succeed. I'm one of the few who did and one of the majority who failed. I had a little money in the bank after I departed Bear Stearns. I was looking for something to do. One day I stopped by a shopping center and saw a man pressure washing the sidewalks. His work was slipshod. I noted that he was missing plenty of spots. For some reason, I felt the need to talk to him. I don't have much of a filter. I just say what comes to mind. I pointed out the spots he had failed to clean and asked how much money he was getting paid to wash the sidewalks. He was kind enough to tell me. I asked him how many hours it took. He was getting a little uncomfortable with my audacity and the troublesome line of questioning, but he told me anyway.

I did the math and calculated that he was making a whopping $75 an hour. The minimum wage at the time was $3.35. It didn't take long before I began looking into my own pressure washing business.

I did everything wrong. I was undercapitalized from the start and had no business plan. That is a double tap right between the eyes and a surefire way to fail. Trust me, I failed hard. I maxed out my credit cards and savings. I purchased an ancient Chevy van with over 200,000 miles on the odometer. I bought a used Hotsy pressure washer, a 500-gallon water tank, and all the hoses and accessories I felt I needed to start.

A month after I began my adventure, the van broke down and the pressure washer bit the dust. I didn't have the money to fix the van nor the washer or to buy new equipment. Silver State Pressure Washing closed its doors before I snared my first client.

I broke two of the most important rules in starting a business. I paid for it, literally and figuratively. I fell flat on my face. I was my own worst enemy, and I took myself right out of the game. As a learning experience, it was invaluable. I learned to never take the quick and easy path, to invest in my equipment properly, to capitalize with an eye toward lean times and slack clientele, to have some experience in the business I was starting, and to have someone on call to give me advice.

When I mention advice, I mean good advice delivered by someone who has been there and done that. Over the years I've read many books and attended numerous speaking engagements on financial success, building successful businesses, and investing. In nearly every event, the speakers and writers failed to deliver usable information. I discovered there was a common denominator in these cases: The majority of those men and women, who offered their sagacious perspectives wrapped in a three-hour pep rally or a 300-page tome, had never owned a successful business! Imagine that. I'd get about the same bang for my buck sitting through a lecture on NASCAR driving delivered by Michael Jordan.

I've owned a lot of businesses over the years. Some made money. Some didn't. Pretty much everyone who makes money will admit that they failed many times before they found a way to succeed and grow wealth. To the person, they'll tell you to have passion for what you're doing and to keep at it no matter what obstacles are placed in your path.

This is critical. YOU CAN NOT GIVE UP! One of the most important keys to success in business is being tenacious. I've known plenty of people who failed and a few who hung in there an extra month, despite the outflow of cash and slack sales, only to see their business take root and rebound.

Here's a second key to remember: If you're entering a business with a partner, conduct a background check on that individual. I don't care whether that person is a buddy, a lover, an investor with deep pockets, or an individual with years of experience in the business. You must investigate them thoroughly. Integrity is critical to the process of doing business.

You can have the best idea, a professionally written and well-thought-out business plan, and a bank account flush with cash. But if you have a partner that is a weak link or has an agenda, you're doomed.

Your partner must have integrity, and you must have trust in that individual. If you go and get in bed with someone who has a broken moral compass, I promise you won't be in business for long. And yes, you can take that to the bank!

Sadly, I have fallen into this trap not once, but three times. Twice I invested a considerable sum of money and my partners simply ran away with the cash. In the third instance, my coinvestor decided the business account was his personal piggy bank. He paid bills and purchased a new car on our dime. Right? WRONG!

Had I conducted a simple background check on any one of these scumbags I would have noted they all had shady pasts and numerous run-ins with the law. One had a history of credit card fraud, one had been convicted of embezzlement, and another had several DUIs and a drug-related charge. If I'd known any of that, I'd have kicked them to the curb and I'd be about $400,000 richer.

All of these individuals appeared to be honest, upstanding people. I'm not easy to fool, and I was taken in not once but three times. I was stupid for trusting in my personal ability to assess character and not doing a basic background check. Lesson learned.

Now when I am approached or asked to invest in any project, I do a complete background check on all individuals involved. And I make them aware up front that I plan on doing so. Not long ago I was asked by a friend to invest in a land deal. We intended to buy a sixty-acre parcel and sell off lots to developers. There were four equal investors in the pool, and each of us stood to take 25 percent of the profit. As the meeting concluded, I told everyone at the table, "Guys, I love the idea and I think we can make a few bucks together. But before I write a check, I'm going to do a background check on everyone involved. I have no problem with you doing one on me. I hope none of you has an issue with that."

As I expected, one of the investors came unglued. He cursed at me. He shouted, "Who the fuck are you to investigate me?" He rambled on for some time, made demands, and accused me of invading his privacy.

Mind you, I had done nothing up to that point. I patiently explained that I had been ripped off several times before and I refused to invest a dime unless I did the proper due diligence on my partners. I was polite and courteous, though the gentleman in question did not deserve my kindness. Eventually, he threatened to sue me and stormed out.

He bailed on the deal of course. I checked him out anyway. This scumbag had spent two years in jail for tax evasion and fraud, and he'd declared bankruptcy several times. His response to a formal background check said everything I needed to know. The deal fell through, which was a positive, really. I saved money on two more background checks.

That said, and with those lessons in mind, we will move on to Chapter Nine: "Fight or Flight." In this war story, I return to *Dual Survival* for a bang-up closeout of this gathering of tales from my life.

9

FIGHT OR FLIGHT

"Sure, the lion is king of the jungle, but airdrop him into Antarctica, and he's just a penguin's bitch."

—DENNIS MILLER

A TALE OF SOUTH AFRICA

I shot forty-two episodes of *Dual Survival*, the most of any host in the seven-season history of the show. We traveled thousands of miles in search of the most challenging and brutal environments on the planet. From the jungles of Sri Lanka to the deserts of Oman to the barren salt flats of Bolivia, I've had to think my way out of situations that would have killed most individuals.

The first thing most people ask me about those years is usually framed as a question within a question: "Why would you do something like that?" The second most asked question is, "Did you really drink your pee?" And the third most asked is, "What place challenged you the most?" The answer to the first question is simple: I love to be challenged. I'm an adrenaline junkie to the core. The opportunity to do something like that was impossible to walk away from. The answer to the second is yes. As I said before, I will do nearly anything to ensure my survival. I felt it was important to make that point clear in my first outing as a *Dual Survival* host.

Finally, I don't even have to think about the answer to the third question. The Kruger National Park, in South Africa, presented the gravest threats to my well-being and pushed me to the very limit of endurance. Walking around in a place inhabited by the most dangerous predators on the planet was an experience I will never forget. It changed how I looked at life. I can't even put that feeling into words. To understand that you really are part of the food chain shakes you to the core.

I remember flying into the park and thinking that it was the wildest, most beautiful place I had ever seen. I was struck by the rawness and brutally harsh landscape and the great herds of Cape buffalo, elephants, and zebra crossing the park's open spaces.

Later, when I stepped out of the Land Rover to start our journey, I felt civilization and its protections slip away. An overwhelming feeling of vulnerability and anxiety hit me hard. I was indeed part of the food chain. There is no more humbling feeling. I had hunted men and been hunted by them. I had survived the worst the human race could throw at me. But I was nearly helpless against an apex predator. The stuff of my nightmares was gliding through the bush just yards away. No amount of training could have prepared me for that environment. I had always marveled at the power and lethality of the predatory cats and the brute strength and ferocity of the African rhino. In an instant, the awe fell away and I knew real fear. I understood that if I crossed paths with one of those beasts, I stood no chance of surviving the encounter.

As we moved down a path, I saw the unmistakable paw prints of a big cat. They were everywhere around us. I recalled that predatory cats rest during the day, eating the kill from the evening before. They're engorged and slow-moving while the sun is out. I concluded that they were unlikely to come at us during the daylight hours. But the idea was cold comfort. I saw numerous lions in the distance. The beasts were shading beneath the spreading limbs of massive baobab trees. They were lazy looking and fat, having recently dined on gazelle meat. The bones were spread out before them like the remains of a savage buffet feast.

Few things in this life strike terror in me. But the sunset in Kruger National Park chilled me to the core. I hardly slept during our stay in that place. The triumphant roaring of the lions and the cries of wounded, dying gazelles punctuated the darkness for hours on end. The noise a gazelle makes while being slaughtered sounds exactly like a woman screaming. It was haunting. It made the hair on the back of my neck stand up. I lay awake all night, on edge, wishing desperately for that first perceptible brightening, for any hint that dawn had arrived, and the danger was passing.

The first two days of shooting were relatively uneventful. On day three the producer decided it was time to film an "Art of Self-Reliance" featurette. This was a thirty-second information plug designed to keep the viewers tuned in. One was included in every episode. In this instance I was supposed to discuss the marula tree, which sprouts a delicious, yellow pear-shaped fruit about the size of a plum. The marula fruit is traditionally used to make a creamy South African liquor called Amarula, as well as jam, moisturizer, and a potent local beer, among other things.

There is a widespread and very persistent myth that elephants eating the rotting marula fruit get drunk and unruly. It isn't true of course. Due to an elephant's great bulk and the amount of water it drinks daily, the animal would be required to eat an extraordinary amount of the fermented stuff to have any sort of an intoxicating effect. I doubt there is enough marula fruit in Kruger National Park to make that happen.

The challenge in acquiring the ripe fruit is that it sprouts from the top of the sixty-foot tree and there are hardly any branches usable for climbing. I decided the best way to get at the food was to fashion a throwing stick and knock it free.

I split from the main group accompanied by a sound engineer and our director of photography. We headed for a distant marula tree that had been spotted by one of our sharp-eyed crewmen.

I led the fifteen-minute hike through the bush. We tired very quickly as the plant life is thick on the ground, thorny and difficult to navigate. We discovered a small, winding game trail that made the trek easier. Naturally, we followed it, making sure to keep the tree in view at all times as we zigzagged and dog-legged toward our destination. Along the way we observed plenty of animal droppings. The spoor left by passing elephants was easily identifiable due to the colossal size of the excrement piles, less so the stool of far-ranging lions and Cape buffalo. After it bakes in the sun for a while, all crap looks and smells the same to me.

We came to a sharp bend in the trail. Due to the man-high grasses blocking my view, I couldn't see what lay ahead. I should have slowed down. I should have exercised a little more caution. But I barreled around that blind curve and found myself facing a massive bull elephant. The beast was a mere thirty yards away. It stood there astride the path, swatting lazily at the ever-swarming clouds of flies with its small whisk of a tail. It saw me the moment I rounded the bend, and its tiny eyes narrowed.

We had received a safety lecture prior to our arrival at Kruger National Park. One of the first lessons we were taught dealt specifically with encountering one of the "Big Five." The Big Five are the most dangerous species of animals in the park. These include Cape buffalo, leopards, lions, rhinos, and finally, elephants. We were instructed to back down slowly and NEVER to turn away or run. Turning your back to an apex predator indicates submission. They will react accordingly and spring, lunge, or trample you. It will immediately stimulate the predator into chasing you down.

I froze like a statue.

Our sound guy didn't see the elephant. Those huge animals have an uncanny ability to blend into the environment. They are the same gray color as the local trees and have dusty hides that match the brown hues of the local vegetation. But he did see me stop in my tracks. Completely missing the gravity of our situation, he joked, "What's the matter, Joe? You lost?"

I turned my head slowly and looked at him.

His amused expression vanished. He was suddenly and rightfully concerned. He had accompanied me into the wild numerous times as we filmed *Dual Survival* episodes. It wasn't his first time in South Africa, and he had developed a nose for trouble almost as sharp as mine. He asked in a low voice, "Are we in danger?"

I nodded. I said softly, "Bull elephant thirty yards in front. He's got his eye on me."

Our director of photography had seen the elephant and understood the situation. I heard him say, "Joe, walk toward us real slow. And don't turn your back to it. Whatever you do, don't turn. You hear me?" I nodded in response.

Then I looked into the elephant's eyes. They were mean, and there was a hint of crazy in them. I know crazy. I've been up against it, and I have a bit in me, or so I've been told. I felt it was important to lock eyes with the beast and keep it off-balance, to make it think I was just as nuts and ready to rumble. It seemed to work. The elephant huffed a little, and its long trunk lashed from side to side aggressively, which I now know is a precursor to attack.

Adrenaline was coursing through me. Tunnel vision hit me fast and hard. All I could focus on was the monster's slowly blinking left eye. Time slowed down.

I looked around to break that intense focus and regain my senses. I recognized with a sinking feeling that the elephant wasn't about to walk away and that the two of us were going to have it out, one way or another. Worse, I saw a pair of elephant calves down the trail. They had been lagging behind the bull and romped into view as I stood there.

They too froze and gazed at the humans blocking the path.

This was a worst-case scenario. A five-ton bull elephant will stand its ground and deal some serious damage if it feels its young are under threat. I was pretty sure we were going to die at that point. I recognized that every second I stood on the "X," my life expectancy was growing shorter.

The beast shook its head aggressively and flapped its ears. I saw those sharp-pointed tusks swinging from side to side. These were all bad signs. We were in very serious trouble. There was no doubt about it. The beast was warning me that it was pissed off and really bad things were about to happen.

I decided to take a step back, to show the creature that I was no threat and planned to retreat.

This turned out to be a mistake. There was no winning that showdown. The massive beast had already decided I was puny and helpless and needed to be pulped underfoot. It had the advantage and knew it.

The monster trumpeted and charged.

I can't put into words what that nightmare looked like. Every hair on my body stood on end. In a matter of seconds it halved the distance between us. Then it closed to within fifteen yards. I remember the odor. The thing reeked. It was like nothing I had ever smelled before.

The elephant looked twice as big as it had a moment before. My overwhelming instinctual response was to take off running like a bat out of hell and climb the first tree I didn't slam into. Resisting that terrible impulse was nearly impossible.

Then my special operations training kicked in. I put aside my fear and did what was required. I stiffened my back and got my wildly dancing nerves under control. I fell back on the instructions I had been given at the start of our South African adventure. I knew that information was right, that it existed for a reason, and doing anything else would mean my end. It would mean I'd be run down and stomped into the ground like a tent peg.

I planted my feet and stared at the charging nightmare. I got my Charles Manson eyes on. I ignored my surging adrenaline. The creature was roaring defiantly. The continuous trumpeting was deafening. I could hear nothing else. Time turned strange and fell out of kilter. I saw the earth pile up in front of the beast as it skidded to a slow-motion halt.

Then, amazingly, the elephant spun around 180 degrees, left the trail, and charged off through the bush. I heard the thunder of its hooves for some time as it barreled through the countryside, knocking over small trees and braying loudly. The calves fell in behind the bull and trotted away out of sight.

I'm reasonably sure I didn't cause the monster to flee. I have no idea what changed its mind about killing me. I was helpless, and we both knew it.

My ordeal ended as quickly as it had begun. I estimate the entire encounter lasted no more than two minutes and probably less. But it felt like twenty minutes to me. My sound engineer guessed ten minutes, and our director of photography said that the elephant and I were facing off for about five minutes. None of us had a firm grasp of the actual time that had passed. No one had looked at a watch. This sort of time distortion is another debilitating effect of an adrenaline dump. In high stress, dangerous situations, it is critically important to manage your adrenaline level as quickly as possible. Take deep breaths, which will help slow your heart rate. Center yourself. Refocus. Your survival depends on maintaining a clear mind and controlling your physical and mental states.

For me, staring down a wild elephant and surviving to tell the tale is an indelible moment in a life filled with adventure. I'll never forget the smell, the danger, and the sheer terror of that unexpected encounter. I was at once the victor over a gigantic and majestic creature, but at the same time, I had never felt more insignificant, small, and helpless.

My survival and that of my crew depended on making the right decision in the moment and having the will and strength of character to do what was necessary. Had I broken and run, like most people would have when faced with such a monster, it is likely all three of us would have died, or at a minimum been seriously injured.

The takeaway from this encounter is that controlling yourself is paramount. It supersedes taking control of an unfolding situation and acting upon the physical world. What's going on in your head will determine whether you live or die, not your fight or flight response or how fast you can run away from trouble. I was not born with this skill. No one is. It must be learned. Mastering it may someday save your life.

Me at a few months old. Little did I know
what my life had in store for me.

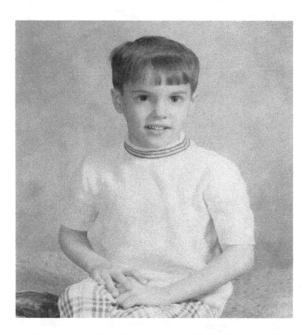

As a young boy I was plagued by phobias of
deep water and heights.

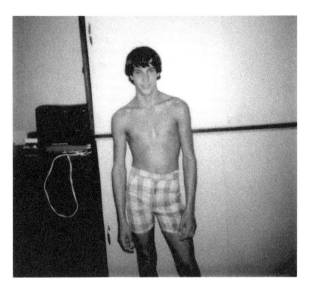

Me in eleventh grade. The proverbial
ninety-nine-pound weakling.

Graduation photo, Marine Corps Boot Camp.
Parris Island, South Carolina.

My first deployment to Afghanistan fighting in the Global War on Terrorism. My rucksack weighed eighty-seven pounds, not counting my assault vest. Being in good shape wasn't good enough.

Post-mission photo. Getting ready to load birds for TST (time-sensitive target). My weapon is a suppressed H&K 416 with a 4x32 Trijicon ACOG and a VITAL 100 IR Laser.

Hunting down bad guys in the Hindu Kush mountains in Afghanistan with Afghan commandos.

Recovery mission for downed MQ-1 Predator, location CLASSIFIED. Note the two Hellfire missiles that did not detonate on impact. We blew them up after recovering all the sensitive items from the crash.

Using a terrain model to brief Afghan commandos on an upcoming night's raid. When your life hangs in the balance, no detail is left to chance. The compound model I am pointing at with the stick was made from pictures of the target building.

On a Yamaha 450 with a suppressed Remington .300 Winchester Magnum. Bikes and ATVs came in handy on certain missions.

Combat diver operations with Draeger LAR-V rebreather.
Little Creek, Virginia.

Rooftop. Advanced Close Quarters Battle training.
Fort Bragg, North Carolina.

Conducting a HALO (high altitude low opening) combat equipment parachute jump at 22,000 feet.

Rode hard and put up wet post-mission picture. This was taken after a seventy-seven hour E&E (escape and evasion). I had not slept in over three days and only had eight rounds left in my M4. I was lucky to be alive. The pilot in the background saved my life and the life of the guy who was with me.

There is more than one way to get to the bad guys.
Going native in Afghanistan.

Pre-mission photo dressed in traditional Taliban garb. Note: Black
Taliban turban. Getting to and from a target was only limited by our
imaginations. Weapon is a Kalashnikov AKMS AK-47.

Some of the beautiful children caught up in the war in Afghanistan.

Hiking in Glacier National Park, Montana.

Paddling in Glacier National Park, Montana.

Cooking up a tiger fish I caught in South Africa,
season three of *Dual Survival*.

My BOB (bug out bag), Afghanistan.

Wondering if I should attempt to drink the water.
Season three of *Dual Survival*, Zambia.

At 17,200 feet, chopping ice with my SURV-TAC 7 in the Atacama Desert in Chile, one of the driest places on the planet.

Minutes after killing a 200-pound wild boar close up and personal with a spear and knife. Season three of Dual Survival, Haleakala National Park, Maui, Hawaii.

Me with Dale Comstock to my right and Mike Donatelli to my left on the set of a new show I was filming. Sadly, this was the last picture taken of Mike—Saturday, February 9, 2013. He was killed the next day in a tragic helicopter accident.

Me with Discovery executive producer, French Horwitz. This was taken on Ometepe Island, Nicaragua, which was my very first episode. French made the long trip and was making sure his decision and Discovery's investment to bring me on board was a good one!

Doing an OTF (on the fly) interview in the Chihuahuan Desert, New Mexico. Season three of *Dual Survival*.

Wild Fire Weekend 2013, speaking in front of a packed BI-LO Center, Greenville, South Carolina. I had never spoken to 10,000 people at once. There is always that next mountain to climb!

Asadabad, Afghanistan

Working out with an elevation training mask.
Simulates working out at 16,000 feet. Great cardio!

I spent ten weeks in Greece. Took a day to go climbing in Meteora. Got to smell the roses every now and then.

In the Hindu Kush mountains, Afghanistan, with members of DEVGRU (SEAL Team 6) and "other assets."

I spent six months as a member of the State Department level PSD (personal security detail) at the US Consulate, Jerusalem, Israel.

Always in the fight! Hauling a freshly killed wild boar out of the bush. I killed it with a spear and knife.

Carpathian Mountains, Romania

Shooting an episode of Dual Survival in the Salar de Uyuni Salt Flats, Bolivia, the largest salt flats in the world.

Hanging off a 250-foot ice crevasse, Briksdalsbreen glacier, Norway.

Hunting for Red Stag on the South Island, New Zealand.
Rifle is a Remington 700 BDL, 7mm Magnum.

Drying out my clothes and a simple shelter for the night
in the jungles of Vietnam.

PART 2
SURVIVAL
A MODERN MANUAL

10

JOE'S TOP TEN RULES FOR STARTUPS

Lesson #1: Develop a Business Plan. If you are going to start a business, you MUST develop a solid business plan. This should be completed before you invest a penny. An actual plan takes the emotion out of starting a business. Everyone thinks they're going to make millions right out of the gate. This isn't realistic. Statistically speaking, half of all startup businesses fail within the first two years. In general, depending upon the situation, I spend a year or more gathering data before I commit to a project. I put together all the information needed to write a business plan. Then I give it to a professional who actually writes business plans.

The average cost for a plan is about $3,000 if you want it done right with all the financial data included. The plan is a roadmap to the future that will prevent overreach and keep you aligned with your starting concept. Most importantly, a properly written plan is a litmus test that will suggest whether your ideas are workable and indeed realistic. If your profit and loss numbers don't gel on paper, they definitely will not work in the real world. If you don't have $3,000 to invest in a professionally written plan, then you shouldn't consider going into business. You're doomed from the start. Finally, if you plan to work with investors, you won't attract one without a business plan, at least one that is for real.

I have spoken to dozens of "investors." In my personal experience, most of them never had the amount of money needed to invest in the first place. Not to sound cynical, but before I share my idea with any investor, I require them to sign an NDA (nondisclosure agreement). This protects your idea from being stolen by unscrupulous people. It's a sad fact, but unfortunately there are some very shady people out there.

Lesson #2: Add 25 Percent to Your Planned Outlay. You had better have enough money to pull it off. Whether you get a loan from a family member, a bank, or private investor, you'd best be sure you have enough cash to cover your expenses and deficits in income and outflow for up to a year. You cannot go back to the well once you ask for money. Being undercapitalized is one of the primary reasons businesses fail. That's a fact. You need to do your homework. You should calculate to the penny what it's going to cost to bootstrap your business. Then you need to add another 25 percent on top of that number **at a *minimum*!** You will never really peg the cost necessary to start a business. There's simply no way to imagine everything.

I spent two years doing my homework on opening a gym. At the end of the day it cost me 32 percent more than I initially calculated. There will always be things you did not account for that will require you to write a check. Depending on the venture, that could add up to hundreds of thousands of dollars.

Let me repeat this. If you figured your fixed and variable expenses to be X, add 25 percent of that total to X. I don't want to be the bearer of bad news, but the reality is, it will cost you much more than you think to open a business, and far more to run it properly. Be prepared and plan accordingly.

Lesson #3: Do Not Get into Business with Someone You Have to Micromanage. This is something I will not do under any circumstances. I am not a micromanager and never will be. To be quite honest, I don't want anyone on my team that I have to babysit. Everyone needs to be a self-motivated and self-starting person. You need rock stars on your team, especially in the beginning stages. One weak link can sink the whole ship. Be superpicky about who you hire early on. These people will make or break you. When you interview potential workers, be sure that you ask questions about their work habits, how they handle confrontation, whether they can multitask and to what level they can take it, etc., etc. One thing I like to do when I speak to possible team members or business partners is to determine whether they are self-critical. I like to ask a jaw-dropper like, "What are your worst three character traits?" True professionals know their weaknesses and are not afraid to verbalize them. We all have weaknesses. If someone responds with, "I really don't know" or "I don't have any," that's a red flag.

Lesson #4: Be Passionate about Your Business. What I mean by that is, you should be in love with what you're doing, not married to a cash-potential calculation. Profit potential is a mythical bird, a moving target at best. You'll never catch it. Unless you're Bill Gates or Warren Buffet, you're going to be disappointed. This is so important. I cannot stress this rule enough. You'll have to work your fingers to the bone for the first year or two to get things off the ground. Waking up in the morning with positive motivation and excitement is where you want to be. When work isn't work, the job will be fun and exciting. That is what will fuel those eighty-hour work weeks. If you crapped your pants when I said eighty hours, get out now. That is what it takes early on in a new business.

Lesson #5: Be Flexible. Even for a guy like me, who is used to preparing detailed mission plans, I still miss things when I map out a startup. I've been shocked by some of my omissions. It's literally impossible to foresee every possible event and calculate all the potential pitfalls and details. If someone tells you they can do that, feel pity for them. They're going to be surprised and overwhelmed by how wrong they are. You must be flexible and able to adjust to unforeseen challenges that inevitably pop up. Using the PACE formula is tremendously helpful. Remember **P.A.C.E.** Always have **P**rimary, **A**lternate, **C**ontingency, and **E**mergency plans in place. This way you can shift gears quickly and efficiently with minimal downtime and interruption. When you get the time, Google MDMP (military decision-making process). There are tons of gold nuggets in the process you can and should use. Not all of it will apply to your venture, but I guarantee you can get some great information out of it. A must-read.

Lesson #6: Don't Be Afraid to Take Risks. I am a risk-taker by nature. Many people are not. I mean no disrespect to the cautious sorts, but it's unlikely they'll ever be hugely successful. Ask any highly successful person about risk and they'll explain, in their own words, that there is no reward without risk. Some will tell you that a bigger risk equals a bigger return. I agree. At this point you need to stand in front of a mirror and take a good, long look at yourself. Ask yourself if you're willing to stick it out there, knowing full well the odds are that it's going to be cut off. I've been there. I've done that. Having your financial head chopped off sucks.

I have a stock certificate in my desk drawer that's now worthless. That ten-cent piece of paper cost me $170,000. I invested a ridiculous amount of money in a company that went belly up in less than nine months. I took a very big chunk of my savings and put it into this deal. I keep that certificate as a reminder. Occasionally I have to remind myself not to be stupid. I've tempered my decision-making process since then. I do my homework before I invest. Look before you leap right into the deep end of the pool. What I mean by this is: DO YOUR FREAKING HOMEWORK. Don't just do a fly by and check all the blocks.

It takes time and effort to really conduct due diligence. This is great advice. But beyond that, don't be afraid to take a risk. No bird has ever flown without stepping off the branch, free-falling, and then flapping its wings. The old adage "a fool and his money are soon parted" is 100 percent true. And I have been that fool a few times. With the ability to data mine almost anything these days, there is no reason whatsoever for anyone to blindly throw their hard-earned money at something or someone without first conducting a detailed due diligence. If you do, you deserve to have a worthless stock certificate in your desk drawer . . . just like me.

Lesson #7: Share the Wealth. I am staggered that some of the largest companies in the USA gross north of 200 billion dollars a year and fail to pay their people a living wage. I guess no one is holding their feet to the fire so they feel free to screw their workers, who, in reality, are their most valuable assets. I personally believe that paying people a fair wage is the only way to do business. Several years ago I hired a general manager to get one of my startups rolling. I structured a lucrative bonus program for him based on performance. A business analyst would tell you that's all sorts of wrong . . . it will affect your bottom line. After all, he had never worked for me so I couldn't say what sort of work ethic he had or whether he was trustworthy and capable. I can tell you this: His work has been solid and impeccable since we signed the paperwork.

Remember, your most valuable assets in business are your employees. If you want to establish real beneficial relationships with them, you must take care of your people financially. This is where you need to control your greed. I know you're greedy. Let's just get that out the way. Everyone is. Sharing the wealth means you'll earn more in the long run. I like to say, "Share the wealth, and feed your greed." Treating your team members fairly when it comes to financial compensation will also promote long-term relationships in your company. Turning over employees is not only time consuming, but costly. To lose a rock star team member to a competitor for another few dollars an hour, or a few thousand dollars a year, is absolutely stupid. I will take that money out of my own pocket every time to keep that person. Personally, I would love to be able to tell people I pay my people a million a year! Life would really be good!

Lesson #8: Obsess over the Details. The saying, "The devil is in the details" is spot-on. In business and life in general, the more detail-oriented you can be, the better things will turn out. Being a bit OCD can actually be a blessing. I have been in business with people who called themselves "big-picture types." All that means is that they don't want to be bothered with the details. They're not especially savvy managers who have a leg up on the rest of us. If they accomplish anything, it's because their employees do it all for them. I cannot and will not operate like that. I want to know the nitty-gritty details. I want to be informed daily. Without information, you cannot possibly make good business decisions.

As in combat, intel drives the battlefield. If you don't think business today is a battlefield, you need to wake up and smell the coffee. Word of caution!!! Do not get what I call Analysis Paralysis. Meaning, you have done so much detailed planning and data mining that you are paralyzed in regard to making decisions or selecting a COA (course of action). Too much information, or worse, superfluous information will cloud your judgment and make it very difficult to get to the execution phase of your venture. Don't be afraid to run your information and data by someone you trust and admire. It is always a good idea to get the opinions of others who are not involved in the plan. They are not emotionally connected to it and will give you nonprejudicial opinions that you may want to use.

On several occasions in Afghanistan we put together a so-called "Green Team." In a nutshell, this consisted of a few operators who were NOT going on the mission. They sat in on our operations order briefings, in which we laid out plans for our leadership. The Green Team sat at the back of the room and listened to the entire brief. Once it was done, they asked questions about certain aspects of the mission that they felt needed more attention or planning. This worked well because they were not involved in the planning process and they were not going on the mission. They had no emotional connection with the people or results, therefore they could look at the plan from a truly impassive viewpoint. This is an excellent tool for anyone planning a big project or event. Form your own Green Team, and listen to what they say.

Lesson #9: Hold Yourself and Your Company Accountable. Let's face it, we all make mistakes. When we do, we need to own those mistakes and apologize for what we did or didn't do. I am sick and tired of seeing companies operate day after day, making mistake after mistake, failing to take ownership of the errors, and running along in full-tilt crisis-management mode. Convey to your client that you made a mistake and you intend to fix it. They'll appreciate your integrity. In thirty years of running businesses I have never regretted owning up to a mistake. To be perfectly honest, I have received more business and good comments from clients and customers because of it.

NEVER place the blame on another employee or team member. That makes you look, one, ignorant, especially if you are the owner of the business, and two, highly incompetent. Many times you will find that owning up to the mistake will be enough to quell any issues. If that doesn't work, be prepared to offer the offended party some sort of compensation. I will give you a great example. I own a small MMA gym in North Carolina. One day a member tried to get into the building with his access card, but it didn't work. My gym is open 24-7 and has an electronic door lock. I checked his account and saw that his card was deactivated because of nonpayment of his monthly membership fee. I learned that my management software had made the mistake, not him. Instead of telling him, "Hey, man, you didn't pay last month's membership fee. Pay and I will reactivate your card," I drove to the gym and let him in. I told him what had happened and apologized for the inconvenience. Little did I know who this guy was. He was the athletic director at a local school. THE NEXT DAY I signed up twenty students as new members.

Lesson #10: Give Back. Far too many successful people do not do this. I find it disheartening and appalling. I am not a member of the 1 percent, but I've made a nice life for myself through hard work and dedication. Whenever I can, I try to give something back. I donate food to homeless shelters. I take clothing to Goodwill, and I make donations to worthy charities when I can. It's my intention to build a homeless shelter for veterans someday. This is something I've wanted to do for years. The ten-million-dollar price tag is a hefty one, but I won't hesitate to get it done when the funds become available to me. I believe we all owe a debt for the gifts we've been given, be it wealth, a loving family, great friends, your health, or just plain happiness. I have been blessed with all of the above to one extent or another.

I believe that doing good for others, and being a servant-leader, is a most rewarding and fulfilling lifestyle. I encourage everyone to try it, even if it's in a small way, like picking up the tab at a restaurant for a veteran and thanking them for their service. You will find the kindness and grace you give to others will be rewarded to you in many other ways in your life. I guarantee it.

I want to close this chapter with this final thought, and it plays into lesson learned #10. It's fine to have a lot of money, a lot of success, and a lot of "things" if that's what makes you happy. I went through that phase. I had to have the big house on the lake, the cars, the boat, and all the toys. But you know what? As you move through life and evolve, you'll discover that gold eventually loses its luster. Don't get me wrong. I still like my toys. But how many cars can you drive at one time? I can tell you that helping the unfortunates among us will give you far more pleasure than buying a new Benz.

In the grand scheme of things, we exist for a blink of an eye. Make use of the time. Give back when you can, become a servant of your fellow man, and trust in the fact that you will be blessed. I know I have been. The Lord sees all and knows we are given the power of CHOICE in our lives. Showing your fellow man a little compassion is one habit I am glad I adopted.

II

TEN RULES FOR SURVIVING AND THRIVING IN THE MODERN WORLD

EVERYONE HAS THEIR OWN "rules" that they live by. My own personal rules are time tested and have worked for me, not 100 percent of the time, but damn near. They aren't terribly specific, but they are solid. I call them my Ten Rules for Surviving and Thriving in the Modern World, and I will spell them out for you in this chapter. These rules do *not* include a list of items most useful in a bug out bag or what supplies you should stash away in the event of an apocalypse. Instead, I'm trying to provide you with a set of useful rules that will get you through your daily grind. Mean bosses and horrible children won't penetrate your calm shell if you live according to these ten essential guidelines. First and foremost ...

Rule #1: Don't live your life by "what ifs." I'm 99.9 percent sure you've said to yourself, "What if such and such would have happened, or what if I had done this instead of that?" Stop it. For starters, there isn't a damn thing you can do to change the past. Decisions were made, and those decisions affected your future in a good way or a bad way. But the past doesn't exist anymore. The future doesn't exist either. You can only live in the moment. Sitting around years later and pondering the "what ifs" is an exercise in complete futility. Additionally, it hurts you emotionally. It hampers you from reacting appropriately to present-day events. "What ifs" are negative. They reinforce and compound your past mistakes. They are a useless exercise in regret.

I refuse to ask the question "what if" anymore. I live a life devoid of regrets. It took me years to teach myself to be this way, but better late than never. You can be sure that living a life without any regret is difficult. But it isn't impossible. It doesn't involve an action in the physical world, like taking a journey or knocking down a door. The change is a mental one. It's literally all in your head.

Throughout life, we choose specific actions and are forced to live with the consequences, good, bad, or indifferent. But opting to live without regret is a choice we make on a different level. It's strictly emotional and intellectual. **We choose whether or not to regret something.** Why shouldn't we choose to put those regrets aside?

Every one of us has done something stupid. If you survived it and learned from it, it made you a better, more evolved person. If you didn't learn from it, if you've repeated the same mistake and still can't understand why it keeps hurting you, then you need to sit back and perform a little self-reflection. Look deep into your personal history, dig up those old bones, and ask yourself, "What if?" What can you learn from it? The point here is that it's okay to ask "what if" when reflecting upon past situations, but we don't want to build a life around "what ifs." We do not want to dwell on the past in a negative manner. Move on, and make the necessary adjustments so history stops repeating itself. You need to get all the "what ifs" out of your system. Are you done now? Fine. From now on, no more "what ifs."

Rule #2: Do not allow negative people in your life, in any capacity. I call negative people "emotional vampires." We all know these folks, these soul-suckers. What I didn't realize until I was well into my forties is how these people held me back. I was so busy supporting and bucking them up that I wasn't as productive or useful as I should have been.

According to medical studies, negative data passed to the brain is *immediately* stored in your long-term memory, in a part of the brain called the amygdala. Positive information and stimuli take a while to become embedded in our memory, about twelve seconds or so. We are predisposed to prefer bad memories and negative thoughts and store them at once. This is a primitive neurological phenomenon. It was likely designed with survival in mind.

In our distant past, pleasant experiences weren't as important as negative ones. When confronting a predator, we needed to know at once what actions would save us, and it was important to store these away immediately. We aren't being hunted anymore. We've moved past that particular phase in our species' existence. But our brains haven't evolved as quickly as our bodies and technology. So we watch a lot of negative news, and our brains reward us with endorphin rushes. Similarly, sitting around and dwelling on our past foolishness makes us feel as if we're accomplishing something. We delude ourselves into thinking we're learning. We aren't learning anything. We're just wasting time feeling sorry for ourselves.

Negative people drain you physically as well as emotionally. There was an individual in my life who was a complete emotional vampire. An hour with that person made me feel as if I hadn't slept in a week. The negative vibes were nearly electric and to be honest, they were frightening. This is an extreme example, but I've met many others who left me exhausted and numb. I am a very positive and upbeat person by nature. Negative people and positive people don't mix. They're like vinegar and oil. They never blend. My point is this: What you let into your mind will have a big effect on you. So start questioning what you allow in.

Ask yourself, what are the top three sources of negativity in my life? Those sources might be people, porn, alcohol, magazines, social media, drugs, lingering memories of ancient mistakes, or something altogether different. Once you identify the top three, you should ask yourself how you can minimize those influences. If you can't find ways to eliminate them at once, then take smaller steps and focus on dealing with one negative soul-sucking vampire at a time. Once you've freed yourself of those influences, you'll find you have more time and energy. Now you should seek out sources of positivity, whether those are relationships, a spiritual guide, or a pet who adores you. Try this for a month and see what a difference it makes. I was told the same thing several years ago, and I can assure you there was a quantifiable difference in my performance, overall happiness, and mental attitude.

Today TV news is about as negative as it's ever been. Although I pride myself on knowing about and understanding current events, I have cut way down on the amount of news I digest. The state of modern media is deeply disappointing to me. It's sad but necessary for me to cut it out of my life. Since I've made this change, I perform at a higher level and I'm more optimistic about life in general.

Lastly keep this in mind: You may have to make some very hard decisions when it comes to ridding yourself of negativity. It may mean doing away with long-term personal relationships. Recently I decided to cut ties with a friend of more than thirty years. I spoke to him first. I talked to him about having positive conversations. I described the negative effects he was having on me. It made no difference. Dark is dark. Negative is negative. Believe it or not, I loved this person dearly as a friend. But guess what? I love me more. That may sound quite cold, but these are the cold facts of either keeping negativity in your life or not. It's your choice.

It may be a hard thing to do, but you must put yourself first. You must cut away the negativity that's holding you back. I promise, it will only make you happier.

Rule #3: Maintain yourself physically. Work Out. Without your health, nothing matters. Spare me your excuses. To me, excuses mean only one thing: You couldn't care less about your health and physical fitness. If that is you, save time right now and skip to Rule #4, because reading this will not help you. NOTHING is more important than your health. Nothing.

Not long ago I had the scare of my life. I was getting ready to start my third season of *Dual Survival*. For insurance purposes I was required to get a full physical prior to starting to film. Part of the physical was a complete blood series. I wasn't worried about anything as I have maintained my health quite well and work out five days a week religiously. Two days after my physical the doctor's office called me. It was the office manager.

From the minute she started talking I could tell something was wrong. All she said was, "Mr. Teti, we need you to come back to the office and talk to the doctor." I asked why. She replied, "I'm not at liberty to discuss it over the phone. You just need to come in and talk to the doctor."

My heart sank. What in the hell could be wrong with me? Of course worst-case scenarios crossed my mind—cancer, diabetes, heart trouble, or a plethora of other ailments I could have contracted during my last two years wandering the planet, living in austere conditions, and drinking shit water out of holes a goat wouldn't touch. I felt the blood drain down to my feet. A cold sweat came over me. Was I dying? I told the woman, "Unless you tell me what this is in regards to, I'm not coming in."

She replied, "We need to discuss your blood work."

That was all I needed to hear. Not good. It was noon on a Wednesday. I set an appointment for Friday morning. I can tell you I did not sleep until after my appointment. The thought of my life coming to an end sooner than expected was mind numbing. It consumed my every thought. I reflected on my life and began to soften the blow that there might not be much time left on my life clock. Here we go with the "what ifs" in a big way. I tried to avoid that, but it was impossible.

I remember looking in the mirror in the morning before I went to the doctor's office. It was so surreal it is impossible to describe. Verbally, I said to myself, "Joe, you have lived an amazing life. If this is the end, so be it. You're right with God. No worries here."

I wasn't scared, only disappointed that I would not be able to accomplish other goals I had set for myself at that time. That Friday morning driving to the doctor's office I remember well. You could have told me I just won the lottery for a billion dollars and I would not have given a second thought to it. The fact that I might be on my way to meet my maker soon consumed me. Money? What's that?

After meeting with the doctor, he told me my white cell blood count was abnormally high. He asked me if I was on any medications. When I filled out my medical exam sheet, it skipped my mind that I was taking anti-malaria pills (Malarone) because the first place we were going was to a location that had a high threat of malaria.

I was supposed to take the pills two weeks prior to leaving and two weeks after I got back—two pills once a day. Well, I was taking four just to be sure. Let me tell you, I know guys who have malaria. They will tell you it is excruciatingly painful. No thanks. I was not going to go down that road. So, I had doubled my dosage. This put the screws to my blood work in a way my doctor was not able to identify. Once I told him, he immediately ordered me another blood workup a few days later after he told me to stop taking that amount of Malarone. Indeed, it was the "overdosing" of the Malarone that had screwed up my test results. I was fine. The point here is simple. NOTHING is more important than your health, not even winning the lottery.

Rule #4: Hold yourself accountable. Own your success and your mistakes equally. Good Lord, these days the word accountability should be a four-letter word. I could spend an entire chapter talking about prime examples of the lack thereof in business, government, and every other facet of life. Somewhere during the past fifteen years, for whatever reason, we have not held ourselves accountable for much at all, even as a nation. I find this deeply saddening.

Being accountable is more than just being responsible for something—it's also, ultimately, about being answerable for your actions. To hold yourself accountable, you must find the motivation to do difficult things. You need to amplify the urgency of your mission, know why it matters, and understand how taking responsibility helps you become the kind of person you want to be. Here are four things I do consistently to hold myself accountable:

Write everything down. This is one thing that I take to the extreme simply because I am a very visual person and it works. I write down everything, from to-do lists to short- and long-term goals, fitness goals, financial goals, and anything else I want to quantify. I like to see them constantly, which allows me to focus on each one individually. I write my daily to-do lists on multiple sticky notes and place them all over my computer monitor and bathroom mirror, and as I complete them, I take them off and toss them in the trash. And NO, I don't make notes on my phone. These notes stare me in the face from the minute I get up, and they are the last things I see before I go to bed. My goal is to get rid of them as quickly as possible every day.

Identify your personal mission statement. I have a very simple mission statement: Work hard, play harder, love hardest. Your personal mission statement doesn't have to be longwinded. It simply needs to define you as a person and define what it is that you are working toward each and every day. This keeps you focused on what is most important to you. Using mine as an example, it explains who I am and what I get out of bed every morning for. Recite it in your head every morning or print it out and hang it in your office. When your mission statement fuels your fire, you know that you have found the right passions and path.

Celebrate your success. I used to never take vacations. As a matter of fact, I went five years in one stretch without a single vacation, not even a weekend getaway. Smart? Actually, it's quite stupid for numerous reasons. I would work nonstop, even on Sundays. It was so unhealthy and had a negative impact on my heath and overall happiness. Once I came to terms with the fact that it is not only okay to take a vacation, but actually beneficial, I started to use accomplishments and milestones as indications of when I would take off and unplug to recharge my batteries, physically and mentally.

Although I still take vacations, even though I have been all over the world (sixty-three countries and counting) and forty of the fifty states, these days I reward myself a bit differently. It's not a monetary thing with me. I now celebrate my small victories along the way instead of waiting for that big home run. I do small things, such as an extra hard workout on a day that I didn't feel like working out. I will treat myself to a nice dinner. Or I will finish a book (I read REALLY slow) faster than I expected. Any small victory I accomplish, I reward myself—with even something as ridiculous as going for a ride on my Harley.

I have a friend, a very, very successful friend, who owns a large real estate firm. He probably has 500-plus agents working for him. This man has not been on a vacation in ten years, I bullshit you not. It's certainly not for lack of money. He makes several million dollars a year.

When I asked him why he didn't vacation, his answer was bewildering. He said, "Joe, it took me fifteen years to build this company up. I can't leave for a day. Things won't get done."

Are you freaking kidding me! This is a piss-poor reason not to celebrate your success. Additionally, if your employees are so poor they won't work without you shadowing them, then you're admitting failure on a lot of levels.

I told him, "When you die, you're going to have a thirty-million-dollar funeral!"

Create microgoals. I love these! Microgoals are seldom discussed and rarely practiced. When you identify several smaller goals and commit to hitting each one, it keeps you accountable in terms of the overall success of the end goal. I have read a lot of books and attended far too many motivational seminars about goal setting and performance. Goal setting is an absolute must to top performance. And far too many times, these speakers or writers fail to establish the importance of creating microgoals. Simple example: You are forty pounds overweight. Your "goal" is to lose those pounds and tone up. Great! Easy day, right? Wrong!

Having goals is important. It is important to achieving personal and professional success and overall happiness. But sadly, many goals go unaccomplished. In my opinion, one of the major causes of failed goals is the lack of urgency. When setting goals, we tend to think too much about where we will be in the future and not enough about what we need to do now to get there. And while it is important to visualize future success with our long-term goals, something needs to be done at the present to get there. There needs to be a tangible link between the future and the now. Ergo, microgoals.

Microgoals are simply your long-term goals broken down into everyday minigoals, or mini-milestones. They can also be seen as subgoals. Microgoals are extremely specific—they are task-specific goals and deal with everyday tasks that need to be done in order to achieve bigger goals. Here is what a microgoal looks like when it's broken down from its larger goal:

Long-term goal: Lose thirty pounds in ninety days.

Short-term goal: Run at least two miles a day, every other day for the next sixty days.

Microgoal: Get to the gym and run at least a mile **today**. Then once you are finished with that first mile, your next milestone is to add a mile on each week after the fifth week.

Microgoals break down any task into smaller steps. A goal of running two miles today is a short-term goal. But a microgoal breaks down those two miles into smaller chunks so that it will push you to just start—and to keep going once you've started. While two miles may not seem like much to a seasoned marathon runner, it is a mountain for those who are not accustomed to running at all.

When I attended SFAS (Special Forces Assessment and Selection) I knew going in that more guys failed the course than passed. One of the best pieces of advice I was given prior to leaving for SFAS was to set microgoals every day. They were simple: Wake up and make it to breakfast. Make it to lunch. Make it to dinner. I did that day after day until I graduated. There is no way that you can eat an elephant without taking small bites. These were quantifiable, in my face, everyday successes. It worked, and I can tell you there is no way I would have made it through such a physically abusive course without setting microgoals. No way.

Rule #5: Review your performance. As a performance-oriented person, it's important that I am brutally honest with my performance. In the end you are the one who is responsible for your success or failure. Do not be that person that blames others for lack of performance. Sorry, that dog won't hunt. I'm constantly reviewing my own performance, and I'm not afraid to tell myself when my performance is not up to par and if I am dragging my feet.

If you really want to be held accountable, constantly keep yourself in check. As a business owner, if you start to slack and your sales slow and business is down, there isn't anyone to blame but yourself. Oh, by the way, CEO means CHIEF executive officer. If you can't live up to the title, you're in the wrong position. Fire your ass and hire someone that can take the heat.

A business owner that blames others is destined to fail because he or she would rather point fingers rather than review their own performance. I have a very simple system I use on a weekly basis that lets me review my performance for that week. It is based on the microgoals and goals I set for myself that week, how well I accomplished them, how I dealt with adversity and challenges that popped up, etc.

I use a simple one-to-ten ranking scale, and I can assure you that I don't stack the deck. I am extremely hard on myself, always have been. You have to be able to look in the mirror and give yourself a verbal ass beating for not performing to your ability. I promise you, if you can be brutally honest with yourself, that is a huge step in personal growth on several levels.

Wake up every morning with at least two to three goals you want to accomplish. If you are not moving forward, you are moving backward. Be they small or big, get in the habit of accomplishing something positive every day, seven days a week, 365 days a year. It's just that simple. Establish a habit of winning small battles every day, regardless of how small or mundane they may be. This will start to train your brain on a "win everyday" mindset. We will be talking about that more later on in this book.

Rule #6: Keep your emotions in check in all you do. It's no secret that emotional decisions tend to be the worst ones you can make. I don't need to get into the psychology of why, let's just get to the point here and understand it's a bad idea. Have I done it? Yes. Did those decisions work out to my benefit? Hardly. Let's face it, it would be cool to be like Mr. Spock on *Star Trek*, but we are human beings and just can't turn off our emotions like a light switch.

As performance-oriented individuals, we've all been in situations where we let our emotions get the best of us. We get so caught up in the drama of things that we let our feelings control our decisions, which unfortunately pulls us away from our goals. When I find myself in a similar situation, I ask the following questions:

1. Do I have any feelings associated with the situation that may negatively impact my decision?
2. How will this decision ultimately impact my life, relationship, or business?
3. Once I make this decision, how long will it take to achieve my expected result?

Number one is really important because there have been many times that my "feelings" were only perceived feelings, not real raw emotion. I got caught up in the moment and let other people wind my clock and spin me up emotionally and set me on a path I had no business being on. I am sure you can relate. Avoid this type of situation at all costs. If that means walking out of a meeting that is going south, do it. I was in a meeting several years ago at an attorney's office. It was me, my attorney, and several others.

It was very apparent that these other attorneys representing one of the business entities involved in a real estate deal I was involved in had an agenda. For whatever reason they were trying to get me to bow out of the deal. They were saying things to me to try to upset me. Even my attorney knew it.

My blood was starting to boil from their comments and criticisms of my lack of experience in such a large real estate deal. They told me that I brought too much risk to the table in the form of what they called "significant lack of real-world experiences in regards to a transaction like this."

My attorney saw that I was starting to lose it. And that is what the other attorneys wanted. They were setting me up emotionally to throw in the towel. I found out later that one of the attorneys had another investor lined up (a friend) who wanted in on the deal. Unethical? Just a bit. But I was onto them. I quietly and professionally excused myself from the room, walked to the bathroom, splashed some water on my face, and took a five-minute break. I did some basic mediation therapy in one of the toilet stalls and headed back to the conference room for round two.

But this time I had a plan and was in control of my emotions. Their plan failed, and I invested in the deal with a few others and did quite well. That one deal would have cost me a ton of money, which turned out to be my bankroll for future deals to come.

Bottom line, keep your emotions in check at all times. When you need to remove yourself from a bad situation and regroup, do so.

Rule #7: Hope for the best, plan for the worst. Here again some people may question this "attitude" of planning for the worst. But let me tell you that I am here today because of this philosophy. During my tours in Iraq and Afghanistan, I conducted many missions. I can assure you that every single one was planned with meticulous attention to detail.

Now let me ask you this question: Considering that your life is going to hang in the balance between the planning and execution of these missions, would you expect that everything would go according to plan? The answer is absolutely no. I honestly don't remember conducting a mission and coming back and doing our "hot wash"/ debrief and everyone saying, "Wow. It went just like we planned!"

Does that mean we didn't plan accordingly? No. The fact of the matter is that in life, like combat, Murphy's Law applies. For those of you that have never heard of Murphy's Law, it is an adage or epigram that is typically stated as: "Anything that can go wrong will go wrong."

So, back to that small detail about your life hanging in the balance. Knowing that there will be things that go wrong, regardless of how well you have planned, you MUST plan for the worst-case scenario.

A perfect example of this is the raid that killed Osama bin Laden on May 2, 2011. It was code named Operation Neptune Spear. The units involved with this historic mission represent the "elite of the elite" in US special operations. They have conducted thousands of missions over a period of many years hunting down terrorists all over the world. It goes without saying that the mission to kill bin Laden was meticulously planned.

While deployed in Afghanistan I worked with members of both Gold Squadron and Red Squadron of DEVGRU (SEAL Team 6). These guys are a Tier 1 Special Mission Unit that conducts the most sensitive missions assigned to the US military.

Red Squadron was sent in to kill bin Laden. These guys had several weeks to practice day and night on a real-world mockup of bin Laden's compound in Abbottabad, Pakistan. Every possible contingency was rehearsed and accounted for. Like all other special operations units, they plan for the worst. And the worst happened.

For those of you not familiar with the mission, one of the two stealth Blackhawk helicopters crash landed inside the compound. Can you plan for such a catastrophic event? Yes. Did they? I am sure there were contingencies in place for just such an event. It might have been an abort criteria for a lesser trained and experienced unit. However, these guys are true professionals and their real value is their ability to continue with the mission even after a major failure in the plan, like a helo crash. Most units would have been out of the game right there. The pilot saved the day and nosed the bird in without it tipping over or injuring any of the SEALs on board.

I always look at any business opportunity or project through the eyes of "what is the worst thing that can happen." I can tell you this, (great quote): "Fail to plan, plan on failing."

Rule #8: Develop and cultivate a warrior mindset. I wish I had a dollar for every time I did a speaking engagement and mentioned the warrior mindset, then heard some accountant, doctor, or office manager say that they didn't need any such thing. After all, they weren't going to war. Right? The funny thing is, a person with that attitude is exactly the one who needs it.

It's not about going to war or into combat, like most people think. I've been featured in several magazine articles about my experiences and the warrior mindset. I hate the word expert, because 99 percent of those who call themselves one aren't. I don't consider myself an expert at anything. But I do know a bit more about certain subjects than most. As you know from an earlier chapter in this book, I'm a huge proponent of the warrior mindset.

So, the first question you may be asking yourself is, "Am I born with a warrior mindset?" That's a tough question to answer. I say that because the warrior mindset is a skill that is cultivated as we mature. Some people cultivate it at a very early age. In many cases those who do were kids pushed really hard by their fathers in sports. I certainly did not have this skill in high school as I was not an athlete. The warrior mindset is highly prevalent in contact sports like football, hockey, wrestling, martial arts, etc. Most of us have heard the term *warrior mindset* being used quite a bit in recent years, with very little explanation as to what it really is.

Well, a true warrior mindset is the original way of creative problem-solving and "thinking outside the box," to be perfectly honest. A look into human history will provide you with countless examples of this. Successful warriors from the beginning of time have demonstrated ingenuity, creativity, fanatical discipline, and unique value systems that have been carried on into our modern-day society.

But what is a *warrior mindset*? There are countless definitions of the term. The concept can mean something completely different to people based on their age, experience, or background. Generally speaking, however, the term is most often associated with the mindset of those who place themselves in harm's way by choice such as military personnel and police officers. That being said, you don't have to be a cop, Special Forces soldier, or Navy SEAL to have a well-developed warrior mindset. This mindset is more than aggressive action and determination. It is about overcoming challenge and adversity. It's about possessing, understanding, and utilizing a set of psychological and physical skills that allow someone to be effective, adaptive, and persistent in the most unforgiving circumstances.

It also allows someone to use optimal decision-making skills under extreme stress and pressure when most would just fall apart. To develop a truly formidable warrior mindset will take time and learned skills in training and by experience. In many cases, people are consistently encouraged to maintain their mental focus and to utilize a warrior mindset. However, the kick in the head is that most are rarely ever trained on HOW to actually accomplish that task. Regardless of the definition, real warriors have always been encouraged to train like they are going to fight and accumulate both mental strength and physical strength. One without the other is a losing proposition. In today's modern military and law enforcement communities, it is often assumed that mental toughness will magically generate or automatically result from tough physical and tactical training.

This could not be further from the truth. As a matter of fact, it usually isn't true at all, but mental toughness skills can be trained like any other skill. To develop the true warrior mindset, you must work to develop a mental training program. You must be open to learning and eliminate mental roadblocks.

You must, in a sense, break yourself down just like military boot camps do when new soldiers enter into the military and then you must build yourself back up. The ability to become comfortable with being uncomfortable is a perfect way to look at it.

Rule #9: Practice, practice, practice. One of my favorite sayings is, "Amateurs train until they get it right. Professionals train until they can't get it wrong." Trust me, there is a lot of truth in that saying. In my early twenties I lived in Las Vegas with a close cousin that I mentioned earlier in this book. He had lived there for years and was a percussionist with a few big acts like Wayne Newton and Sammy Davis Jr. Jack was a highly accomplished musician. He attended both the prestigious Eastman School of Music in Rochester, New York, and the Curtis Institute of Music in Philadelphia, Pennsylvania. Jack played every percussion instrument there was, from the drums to the marimbas to the xylophone. You name it he played it, and he played it well.

This guy was at the top of his profession and had been for many years. Regardless, he practiced every day, seven days a week. On occasion I would watch him practice. I was amazed at the "drills" he would do, over and over and over. It wasn't uncommon for him to practice for three hours straight without a break.

Even after serving as a Recon Marine and training hard for years, this was different. It was a whole different level I was watching. Don't get me wrong, I loved my time in the Marines, but now after serving in a unit that is at the "tip of the spear" in special operations, I can see that the training I was doing in the Marines was not the be-all and end-all. No disrespect intended. Just a fact.

Although Jack never served his country, his dedication to practicing his trade was extraordinary. Even to this day I think about it. Here's the bottom line, folks: If you want to be average at a given skill or trade, minimal practice will be needed as you do it enough to be effective. Fuck effective! Mediocrity sucks! And I can assure you if that skill was a deciding factor on your survivability—you know, life and death stuff—mediocrity would get you killed for sure.

I for one don't want to be mediocre at anything I am passionate about. And being a bit OCD doesn't hurt! Take pride in your trade or craft. Be the very best you can be. To do that, you must practice continuously and to standard.

Raise the bar, do not get complacent. Case in point: When I served in the government counterterrorist unit, they sent me off to train with Jerry Barnhart. Jerry is one of the most accomplished and skilled competitive pistol shooters in the world. I trained with him for two weeks. My goal was to shave 2/10ths of a second off my draw time. You read that right: 2/10ths of a second. Last but not least, if you remember anything I just said, remember this: The saying "Practice makes perfect" is bullshit. "Perfect practice makes perfect."

Rule #10: Crawl, walk, run. As we attempt to get better at any given skill or occupation, we need to remember that Rome wasn't built in a day. There are many gaps between what we currently do well, and all the things we'd *like* to do well.

Common sense dictates that there should be a logical progression toward closing gaps and building capabilities in one's life. To get from point A to point B in a skill, I utilize an oft-touted military-training metaphor: crawl, walk, run. Before you can walk you have to crawl, and before you can run you have to walk. So, what the hell does that mean? It's actually quite simple. I will defer to one of the skills I possess and one I continually maintain, shooting.

Take, for instance, shooting a pistol. What is the very first thing you should know about this? You should absorb a lesson on firearms safety. You should learn how to handle a weapon without shooting someone. Kinda important, don't you think?

Accidental shootings happen. "Oh shit, I thought it was unloaded!" You want to avoid that particular scenario. An accident on the range is never good. I have seen them firsthand. It's ugly.

What else? You might want to learn how to disassemble a firearm and clean it. Finally, you need to master the Seven Fundamentals of Shooting. This would be your crawl stage. In my opinion it is the most important stage of all as everything is built upon this foundation. If your crawl stage is flawed, you can rest assured that when you get to the walk and run stage you are going to be behind the power curve.

In the shooting example, the walk stage would look something like this: drawing from the holster, magazine changes, controlled pairs, etc. These are skills that come naturally in the progression of learning how to shoot a pistol.

Lastly the run stage would contain things such as shooting at multiple targets, shooting while moving, clearing malfunctions, etc. Trust me when I tell you, if you can't competently change a magazine, there is no way you will be able to clear a malfunction.

Regardless of the skill you are trying to get better at, you would be a fool not to use the crawl, walk, run progression. Keep this in mind. If you truly want to get better and more proficient, do not rush the process. As a matter of fact, when you think it's time to move to the next phase, don't. Give it a bit more time to really establish that muscle memory.

On that note, can you guess how many times you have to repetitively perform an act to establish muscle memory? There are a wide range of answers to the question. But in my personal experience, you must repeat an act 30,000 times to make it reflexive. For those wanting to rise to top performance in a given skill, the crawl, walk, run progression is the way to go.

12

RELATIONSHIP SURVIVAL: THE FOUR PILLARS

WHEN I CONSIDERED WRITING a book that was part biography and part survival manual, I thought carefully about what information to include. My original plan did not contain a chapter on relationships. I'm not a relationship expert or even remotely qualified to give advice about romantic affairs. I have had dozens and dozens of failed relationships, including a marriage that went bust. Frankly, it's the last thing I want to discuss. But after speaking with a few very close friends, I decided to address the subject. Relationships are highly personal and each one is very different. I can only address MY experiences. The lessons I learned may or may not apply to you. If you get something out of this chapter, great! If not, please feel free to disregard my advice. And don't send me hate mail. That said, I want to discuss what I feel are key points in building a long-term, successful relationship.

I have failed miserably many times at this. I freely admit, I caused some of the breakups. The rest were caused by my partners, though many of them would be disinclined to take responsibility. The old adages are true: It takes two to tango, and there are three sides to every story—your side, their side, and the truth.

My views and opinions about relationships have changed over the years. So, let me start with this. A real relationship isn't built on how many things you find attractive about your partner. Rather, it hinges on how well you handle your partner's negative traits. We all have downsides and negatives, even really attractive women. I know. It's hard to believe. I've dated more than a few of them. And trust me, looks aren't everything. At one point, many years ago, beauty and symmetry were the qualities I valued most in a partner. I wasn't completely wrong to enjoy those things. I still appreciate a beautiful woman. Let's face it, if you are not physically attracted to the person you are with, your relationship is doomed from the start. NEXT!

With that in mind, you have to look deeper. He or she may be drop-dead gorgeous. They might have a body right off the cover of a fitness magazine. But batshit crazy could lurk in that temple of fleshy goodness. Your goddess or god might do hardcore drugs, smoke like a chimney, drink like a fish, have a violent temper, and sleep around like they just got out of prison. At that point good looks and a killer body won't cut it. I dated a long string of adorable losers who did all those things and more. I didn't put up with any of it for long. Some things are just deal-breakers.

You have to set limits and boundaries and discuss them up front with your partner. If they repeatedly step over those lines, you need to let them go. You need to release that pretty thing back into the wild. A person's behavioral patterns are set at seven years old. They will change very little in the ensuing years. They might learn tact and diplomacy. They might figure out when to shut up. But who they are isn't going to change. This is a really important point to remember. They can hide their true nature for a little while, but not forever. Eventually, they'll show you their true face. If you can live with it, great. If it terrifies you, move along rapidly.

I'm going to address the guys first and the ladies next. This has nothing to do with gender or bias. It's just the way I roll. Guys, listen to me. Do not fall into the 80/20 trap. What I mean by this is simple. Do not fall in love with 20 percent of a person. She might be smoking hot and incredible in the bedroom. She might have beautiful blond hair and a velvety voice that sends shivers up your spine. But that isn't who she is. She might look like an angel, but she isn't. She's human, and humans are messy. You can't overlook the things that get under your skin because she has amazing green eyes and knows how to use them. If you make that mistake, you'll pay and pay and pay. To quote a dear friend of mine, "The screwing you're getting now isn't worth the screwing you'll get later." Truer words were never spoken.

Ladies, let me explain something to you. Guys are not mysterious, and they do not run deep. We are who we are. What you see on the outside might seem really attractive. I understand the temptation to imagine there's a prince lurking somewhere inside that fit, muscular body. But there isn't. Unless you date Prince Harry or Prince William, you're not going to get a prince. I think they're both taken, so you're all out of luck. We fellas have a lot of shortcomings. Let's just get that out there on the table. What I want to stress most is, you can't fix us. You can't make a man into a prince. You can try, but he won't change and you will just come off like a domineering, controlling you-know-what. Remember, our behavioral patterns are set in stone in childhood. We are much less complex than you. Bear that in mind when you meet the hunk of your dreams.

With that said, if you can deal with the negative aspects of a person, you are setting yourself up for a successful long-term relationship. The reverse applies to you. Can they deal with your crap? It's critically important that you find these things out quickly. Life is too short to waste.

I want to address cheating here. Listen to me. Most men . . . let me say that again . . . most, not all, *have* cheated or *will* cheat given the proper motivation and situation. It's fact, not fiction. The reasons for this behavior are fairly simple. Race, creed, and financial status have nothing to do with it. Your man will spout excuses when caught. Some are designed to make you feel guilty. Some are meant to elicit your pity. Some are just excuses for inexcusable behavior. But the truth is that maybe his sexual fantasies were not being met.

You might not want to do the dark or weird things that are swimming around in your man's head. He might not want to tell you about his fleshy guilt-inducing dreams. He might have too much respect for you to demand your participation. But if you don't speak to those dreams, if you don't try to understand what he *really* wants, there will be trouble and you must accept at least some part of the blame.

Make no mistake, I do not condone this behavior. If your man cheats, it is never entirely *your* fault. It's mostly *his*. It's his because he wasn't honest. It's his because he chose a fantasy or a physical encounter over you and your relationship. It's his because he's hardwired to want something different, something exciting and transitory. But at least some of the blame is yours because you didn't meet his needs, and you didn't communicate or create an environment of trust where communication felt safe. Oh Lord, I can see the hate mail already! However, that door swings both ways. If your man isn't making your toes curl, shame on him.

If the pair of you do not communicate, you will fall apart and nothing can save you. When that happens, you must examine your part and accept responsibility for the failure.

It all comes down to communication and desire. You desire respect, empathy, and kindness in bed. He's looking for searing hot flesh and blinding pleasure. If some middle ground isn't reached, if you aren't both compromising in bed and expressing your rawest desires, there will be trouble down the road. Temptation will come his or your way. Someone will offer to fulfill one of those fantasies they have been nursing. Walking away from that offer is tough for a man, particularly as he ages and feels less and less desirable. I've known many men who fell into this trap. I took that road myself once and paid heavily for my indiscretions and lost a very good woman. I won't make the same mistake again. I encourage you to be open and experimental in your relationship. TALK to him.

If you can't communicate, move on. It's never going to work.

My advice may leave you feeling lonely. I want to say here and now that it's okay to be alone. There was a time when I had to have a woman around, regardless of the good, the bad, and the ugly. I was insecure. I was worried that I would always be alone. Those feelings faded. I came to terms with solitude. Sometimes being alone is good for you. You have the time to think and dream. You should not *need* a companion. You cannot build a relationship on neediness. If you are lucky enough to find the *one*, good for you. If not, let it be. Some things just happen according to plan. Enjoy the quiet while it lasts.

Marital experts and psychologists will tell you that several pillars are present in any strong, successful relationship. These vary from talking head to talking head. For me, the pillars are:

1. *Open Communication*
2. *Trust*
3. *Respect*
4. *Mind-Blowing Sex*

If one or more of those pillars is missing, I know the relationship is going nowhere, and I exit immediately.

I've dated women who are so closed off or simpleminded that they can't be engaged in a normal conversation. If I want that, I'll go drinking with my buddies. If you can't communicate, you're dead in the water. The same goes for men. Idiot males are not attractive to most women. Good eye candy at best.

Trust is critical. You must be able to trust your partner 100 percent. If the trust between you is broken, it can never really be repaired. You might move on and patch things up, but nothing will ever be the same. Doubt will plague you for the duration of that relationship. I've dealt with this situation several times. For me, once a person has broken my trust and my heart, the wounds they inflict never heal completely. I've known people who've caught their significant other cheating not once, but many times. After the third or fourth time, you might want to reevaluate your relationship and your self-worth. You deserve better.

There are situations and actions in which forgiveness is called for. We sometimes find ourselves making poor decisions in a crisis situation or making dumb choices for no particular reason. A second chance is usually the right way to go when your partner commits a mistake. But infidelity isn't a mistake. It's a relationship-shredding choice. Remember that.

For me, cheating is a deal-breaker. There is no second chance. I will never trust that person again, regardless of the situation. Everyone is different. But my inclination is to just end it and be done. For me, it's simple. For many others, it may not be. But just be aware that a relationship without trust is a sham.

Respect is difficult. It can and must be earned, however it must be present from the outset.

I admit, I have issues with regards to this particular pillar. If I have no respect for a person, man or woman, I'll walk all over them. I'm just built that way. I'm not going to spend any time wondering why. It's part of who I am. I *must* have respect for the people I engage with, in relationships or business. This comes in different forms. I think a woman who is a great mother, one who is loved by her kids and protects them at all costs, is extremely sexy. Sadly, I've met several women who were the exact opposite. I don't have any time for them. My logic is that if you can't be a good mother, what can you be to me?

A positive outlook is important to me. I respect that. I don't deal with negative people. I cut them out of my life.

Physical fitness is something I look for. If you can't or won't take care of yourself, then I won't be a part of your life. That tells me you don't respect your own body. Ergo, you have no respect for yourself.

Respect is a building block that must be present in the early stages of a relationship. If it isn't there, then it's simply not going to work, in my opinion.

Finally, the sex should be mind-blowing. Quite frankly, good sex isn't good enough. For those of you that have not had toe-curling, mind-blowing sex, I feel for you. I will keep this as clean and professional as possible. But I want to make this point very clear. Anyone who says that sex isn't really important in a relationship has never had honest, amazing, mind-blowing sex. Period. It is about the physical act, but it is also about forging a spiritual connection. It's about being so close and perfectly fitted that everything flows from your intertwined forms like your bodies were made for each other. There is no more intimate act you can perform with another human being. If the pair of you can't get that right, you're not connected at all and it won't work. We are physical beings. Every one of us has needs. Those needs must be met. Anything less means you are not properly paired up and you will not succeed. Each of us has very specific sexual likes and dislikes. I have mine, and you have yours.

It is IMPERATIVE that both parties are getting EXACTLY what they need, how they need it, and when they need it to be happy and committed to each other. If not, this can be your undoing and lead to very unfortunate and heartbreaking events. Been there, done that. I have had my fair share of sexual encounters over the course of my life. Some have been nightmarish, some just okay. A few have been good. A very, very few have been mind-blowing. I can count them on one hand. Finding the proper partner in and out of the bedroom is a no-brainer for me. It's a MUST for a long-term relationship. Lastly, in my opinion, a man and a woman need to lust after each other, not just in the bedroom but out of the bedroom as well.

I want to add something here about the second pillar, trust. It's directly connected to the fourth. Without trust, you cannot let go in the bedroom. You cannot be uninhibited. Doubt creeps in. The experience loses its luster. It may be fine at first, but the longer the relationship drags on, the worse the sex will become. Eventually, it will stop altogether. This is the end. There is no saving the relationship. You're on the *Titanic*, and it's time to hijack a lifeboat.

Communication, the first pillar, is also a critical aspect of sex. You must communicate with your partner openly and transparently about your likes, dislikes, and what you will and will not tolerate in the bedroom. Without that communication, the sex falls flat and no one is really satisfied. If the needs of one or both partners aren't met, the relationship will fail.

Finally, both people in the relationship must do their best to keep the intimacy fresh and exciting. Busy work schedules, children, and family pressures shouldn't be used as excuses. This loving act is crucial to any relationship and must be maintained and cherished.

13

THE WARRIOR MINDSET

"The mind is the ultimate weapon.
Always has been, always will be."

—JOSEPH TETI

PREPARE FOR WAR

THE BALLOON HAS GONE UP. The once distant drums of war now keep you awake at night. Your survival hinges on every move you make. Those closest to you rely on your knowledge, strength, and single-minded purpose to meet the next sunrise. This is the scenario you fear most, the one that gnaws at you always, subtly, down deep in your gut.

The idea that you might face overwhelming, long odds of survival without any protection is nearly unthinkable. "It won't happen," you reassure yourself. But it will. At some point in your life, at a moment's notice, you will find yourself engaged in a war whose outcome will certainly determine your fate and likely that of your loved ones.

The challenge you face will be a very personal one. It might involve bullets, disease, hunger, human violence, or even a household accident. A vast and unpredictable catalog of calamities exists that can tear your world apart in an instant. Nature will test you. Whether you survive or perish is entirely up to you. In the end no politician on a distant hill or policeman sworn to protect you will step forward. In the end you will fight your own war, alone.

Whether you find yourself engaged in direct combat or struggling to acquire food and shelter in the wilderness, you will be at war. The fight will be an epic one without an assured end. Only preparation, knowledge, and strength of purpose can turn the tide in your favor. Only you can save yourself and your loved ones. You must prepare for war. You must do it now!

It could happen in a variety of ways. It could happen in the blink of an eye. You could find yourself stranded in a remote and hostile region without supplies. You could be thrust into battle in a distant land, or even at home. Unrest in the inner cities and suburbs could boil over. A terrorist attack could shut down the national power grid. A major storm could devastate your community and place you, as well as those you love, in deep and instant peril.

Civilization as we know it is a thin veneer shielding us individually from the age-old fight for dominance and food. I enjoy the idea of civilization as much as anyone, and I relish its luxuries just like you do. But I also recognize that the order we've built is fragile and it *will* fail.

The Romans of Trajan's era could gaze out upon an empire spanning 2.5 million square miles. They were protected by the largest, technologically advanced fighting force the world had ever known. Unlike the rest of the planet's citizens, the Romans enjoyed clean water, an overwhelming abundance of food, and medical care that vastly extended their lives. The citizens of Emperor Trajan's Rome never seriously imagined that the walls would fall, the legions would evaporate, and their pampered descendants would be slaughtered on the cobbled streets of the City of Seven Hills by foreign invaders.

I ask you now, where is the Roman Empire? Where is the civilization those men and women built with such painstaking care and sacrifice over a period of a thousand years? Where are the Persians? Where are the Athenians and the Spartans? Where are the Mayans and the Incas? For that matter, where are the imperial Britons and the globe-girdling, monolithic Soviets? Civilization will fail you, and it will fall. You can damn well count on it.

The human capacity to band together to share ideas, tasks, and protect one another has lifted us above every other species and ensured our species' survival. But the tribal instinct is, in truth, a weak one. While we are social animals, we are physically and mentally designed to fend for ourselves. We are lone wolves, each and every one of us. We are singular islands of flesh and blood and ideas. When stripped of civilization's good graces and protections we quickly revert to our basic nature. We will scrap like any other animal for sustenance and, like any other, the weak will die and the strongest among us will prevail.

I cannot repeat this enough times or say it with enough emphasis: Civilization will fail.

In a national crisis, the banks will shutter and your money will vanish. The supply chains will break down soon thereafter, emptying the grocery stores for weeks or months to come. In a personal survival scenario, the elements and animal or human predators will test you fully. The layer of civilized fat you now own will vanish quickly. Your physique will be eroded to skin and bones in a matter of weeks. In each and every described instance, the result is the same. Your safety net is gone. Your survival is entirely up to you. You are fully at war.

If you are unprepared, you will succumb. Expect no rescue. Expect no quarter. Depend only on yourself. Fight like hell with every option, tool, and prized bit of lore and knowledge that you possess. Other human beings cannot be relied upon fully, if at all. In a real survival situation, your experience, intelligence, and spirit are your most crucial assets. In other words, we're talking about your mindset.

Though it has been written about by many authors and discussed extensively by military and survival professionals, *mindset* is almost never recognized as the *key* to survival. I argue that it is the single most important tool you possess and the one that will decide your fate. Forget muscle, fire-building technique, and weapons mastery for the moment. Mindset outstrips them all in importance.

A proper survival approach fully utilizing your know-how and harnessing your fighting spirit is what I call the *warrior mindset,* which we have already discussed. It is the first topic I broach when teaching survival classes. The concept and execution of preparedness coupled with mental strength has saved my life numerous times. It is woven through every other chapter and lesson in this book. It is the core upon which all my teachings rest.

I had no difficulty deciding which chapter to make first in this small, easily digestible but vital manual. If you read no further than Chapter One, or you decide to eat the pages for nourishment, at least you will absorb this key lesson. The warrior mindset is the *key* to your survival.

"You can live three weeks without food, three days without water, and three minutes without air, but you won't last three seconds without the will to survive."

— JOSEPH TETI

THE WARRIOR MINDSET EXTENSIVELY DEFINED

The term "warrior mindset" is easily and very often misunderstood. It seems to indicate that one must have combat experience, or at the very least know something about being a soldier, in order to embrace a battle-ready ethos. Nothing could be further from the truth. An accountant who works in a nice air-conditioned office wages a daily struggle for survival. While his or her eight-hour fight may not be as intense and brutal as combat in the field, I assure you that it is equally real and the implications are just as serious to them. An accountant is as much a warrior as any soldier I've met.

It would be useful at this point to define the term "warrior." A warrior does not necessarily wear a uniform or wield a weapon. A warrior does not always require specialized military training. A warrior docs not need to strike fear into the hearts of his or her enemies. I find a wider use of the descriptor is more relevant in real life. I like the definition preferred by the US Army and taught to the students of its Command Values program.

> **War·ri·or** *n.—One who is engaged aggressively or energetically in an activity, cause, or conflict.*

This is a virtuous, simple, and strong description that goes right to the heart of the matter. The daily struggle for bread and rank makes warriors of us all, whether we are US Army Rangers or accountants waging a never-ending battle to balance the books and complete the month ends. If you have reached adulthood and you are in charge of your future, you can call yourself a warrior.

But naming yourself something and fighting hard simply isn't enough. It won't ensure your survival. When the rubber meets the road, a talent for correctly tallying up the numbers won't buy you one more minute of life, nor will a well-honed ability to break down and reassemble a weapon quickly. Even superior firepower and tactical advantage are secondary to the singular critical factor in every life and death struggle. This dynamic is called "will." Your will, and by definition "determination," is the factor that will turn the tide of battle in your favor. This segues nicely into the second term that we must define and understand in order to embrace the warrior ethos, *mindset.*

A *mindset* is broadly defined as "a habitual or characteristic mental attitude that determines how one interprets and responds to given situations." For instance, if someone points a gun at you and your first instinct is to give up and beg for mercy, your mindset is one of surrender. You're probably going to die. If your instant reaction is to leap forward like a comic book superhero and try to take the gun away from your attacker, your mindset is stupid. Again, you're probably going to die. But if you immediately run through a preordered list of options in your mind and choose the one that capitalizes on your enemy's weaknesses, like remaining calm, making eye contact, maintaining the psychological edge, and studying every detail of the victimizer's makeup, you have a survivor mindset. You already know that if the gunman wanted you dead, he wouldn't be holding you at gunpoint. That would be a complete waste of his time. You already know that he wants something, and you can leverage that need to your advantage. By selecting the correct responses, you have maximized the chances that you'll live to see another sunrise. There are many mindsets to choose from. But for our purposes, the survivor mentality is the one we need to cultivate and bring to bear in life's everyday struggles.

Defining "warrior" and "mindset" separately is certainly instructive and useful. But combining the two terms has real power. Understanding the *warrior mindset* as a survival concept and a tool is crucial. According to most studies, success in any endeavor, whether pitching a baseball or surviving a mugging, is directly related to psychological preparedness. Maintaining a can-do attitude, refusing to give in, and truly believing you can succeed is all-important. The key word in that last sentence is *attitude*. You must maintain the proper attitude in order to survive. Navy SEAL and author Richard Machowicz wrote, "Being a warrior is not about the act of fighting. It's about being so prepared to face a challenge and believing so strongly in the cause you are fighting for that you refuse to quit."

Simply put, the *warrior mindset* is defined as a *battle-ready attitude*. A battle-ready ethos includes all the terms and factors discussed in this chapter including preparation, depth of knowledge, strength of will, and a firm belief in yourself. Whether you are an accountant, a housewife, or a soldier on a distant battlefield, the warrior mindset will serve you well and will save your life. When the battle comes to your doorstep, you must have this mindset. A combatant imbued with this knowledge and level of preparation is confident in his or her abilities, exhibits grace under pressure, chooses the proper responses to dangerous situations and opponents, and manipulates the enemy's weaknesses to maximize the chances of survival and ultimate victory.

During my many deployments to Afghanistan, I had the privilege to work with many Afghan commandos. Their ability to tap into the warrior mindset when needed is phenomenal. As a people, they've overcome enormous obstacles and sent every powerful empire packing that dared to tread on Afghan soil. They've done so repeatedly with little more than willpower and well-honed battlecraft. Soviet attempts to crush the mujahedeen began in 1979, and their entanglement with the mountain warriors led to a protracted ten-year bloodletting. They called it quits after suffering 15,000 casualties and losing billions in equipment and treasure. Now most Russians refer to Afghanistan as "The Bear Trap," and they'll never set foot in that hellhole again. The defeat of the modern and well-armed Russian army by ragtag and primitive Afghan clans is a classic example of what an underrated, outgunned combatant can accomplish if he has a warrior mindset and his enemy is not prepared to fight such an animal.

The warrior mindset is an extraordinarily powerful tool. You would do well to remember that it is not reserved exclusively for you and me, the good guys. If your enemy has it, he will be formidable indeed. He will be extraordinarily difficult to defeat. He will be your equal in every way. You must bring as much as he does if not more to the fight. You must work hard to sharpen your skills, intellect, and physical condition in advance. You must prepare and maintain the warrior mindset at all times. Unless you are fully prepared when the threat comes calling, you won't survive the encounter.

One of my most vivid memories of combat involves a raid on an Al-Qaeda compound and a bad guy who simply wouldn't give up. The buildings we were assaulting were completely indefensible. We outgunned the enemy by a factor of four. In layman's terms, we carried a bazooka to that knife fight and we used it happily. That afternoon was hot, the sun was bright, and there was nowhere for the militants to hide. While our "target individual" squatted within the dubious safety of a mud-walled hut, his protectors tried hard to bring the fight to us, daring to run into the open and fire back. I gave them plenty of credit for bravery, but it didn't deter my aim much.

Amid all the chaos I noted one particular bad guy who had his head screwed on straight. He had a plan, and he was hell-bent on carrying it out. He was toting an RPG and darting from building to building in search of a good aim point. I knew if he had his way, he would blow the crap out of our nice, secure position.

I raised my M4 to put him down, but my good buddy Larry got there first. Larry was a damn fine warrior, and I will grudgingly admit here and now that his aim and reflexes were superior to mine. He stitched the runner from his right hip to his left shoulder with six rounds. All of them were dead on target. Three struck the man center mass. I saw puffs of dust and dirt rise from his chest and belly as he absorbed the hits. Any one of those terrible wounds would have ended a normal man, one without a powerful survival instinct and a warrior mindset. He went down hard and dropped the RPG, but he wasn't finished fighting, not by a long shot. He proceeded to crawl through the dirt trying hard to reach the weapon and return fire.

I remember looking at Larry, and I'm sure his surprised expression mirrored mine. We were astonished at the man's capacity to endure punishment and his single-minded determination to fight on. He was one tough SOB. Larry put a round in his head and ended the man's personal war against us then and there.

That kind of determination in an enemy is my worst nightmare. The RPG-carrying baddie we left on that remote battlefield exhibited the essence of the warrior mindset. When an opponent gets it into his mind that he's going to fight through you no matter what, when that person is so driven by his convictions that you'll literally have to shoot him to pieces to end the fight, then you've got a serious problem. You're pitted against a threat as big and real as they come. People who can harness this fighting spirit are dangerous indeed, whether they are soldiers or business executives. This quality separates the victors from the losers. If you have it and maintain it religiously, it is far less likely that you'll end up in the latter category. If survival is your goal then you must cultivate and employ the warrior mindset to its fullest potential.

"Learning is not compulsory . . . neither is survival."

—W. EDWARDS DEMING

TAPPING INTO THE WARRIOR MINDSET

Building a warrior mindset is both less difficult and more complex than you might imagine. You don't need to create it from scratch. You already have it. Whether you live in a tough neighborhood or a posh suburb, you have certainly suffered, endured, and prospered. You might not have a brand-new Mercedes, a million bucks in the bank, and a seventy-inch TV, but you're alive, more or less well-fed, and in charge of your destiny. It's not easy to reach this level of existence. Most people never do. The majority stumble through their lives without a single original thought or any desire to mature and evolve. As I said at the start of this book, the fact that you hold this book and have an interest in the contents says plenty about you. You might not know it but you're made of strong stuff. You're far likelier to survive a crisis than your average countryman, and you're also damn lucky.

The statistical wizards at the United Nations estimate that about 108 billion human beings have walked the Earth since we made our debut as a species. Of those, 94 percent are dead. You just won the lottery. You are one of a mere 6 percent graced with life, choices, and freedom of action. I recommend that you turn your face to the sun and enjoy its warmth no matter where you are at this moment. Then I suggest you complete this chapter and begin sharpening the warrior mindset you possess.

Some who happen upon this manual already have a winning spirit and live on a war footing, prepared to do battle at a moment's notice. But most of those turning to these pages for wisdom recognize they can and should do more to improve their survival odds in a crisis. In either case, the knowledge provided here will definitely assist you in recognizing gaps in mental and physical preparation that can hamper performance, leaving you vulnerable to predation.

Some readers have already experienced serious trauma and conflict. If you are one of these, perhaps you've picked up this slim volume hoping against hope to find some medicine that will prevent a recurrence. Trust me when I say this, this book will not cure what ails you. Most human beings who have been victimized are psychologically weakened and insidiously debilitated. The mind and body are distinct entities with different healing rates. While bruises and lacerations vanish over time, almost without tending, mental wounds can linger for decades. A victim of violence must seek and embrace psychological treatment. I cannot stress this enough. You cannot heal mental wounds on your own, and they simply don't get better without the expert application of therapeutic techniques.

Unlike your body, your mind does a piss-poor job of fixing itself. Neuroses and stress disorders only worsen as you move through adult life, adding complication upon complication to a personality already composed of countless layers of experiences and memories, some good and some awful. Like ignored infections, these defects will hamper your performance and attitude and will ultimately shorten your life. Worse yet, by ignoring your symptoms you are literally inviting predators into your life.

Whether you know it or not, no matter how hard you try to pretend otherwise, you openly transmit your mental state to those who surround you. You broadcast who and what you are at all times. While most people don't read these signals correctly and distort them through a lens made of self-centered preconceptions, serial victimizers have an uncanny ability to slice through the fog and recognize easy prey. A rape victim is twice as likely as a nonrape victim to be abused again. Without intervention, a child who has been bullied will be bullied again, no matter the conditions or setting. Without the confidence inspired by a winning attitude and a belief in one's ability to overcome, and without the prompt intervention of a medical professional, victims will remain victims and predators will continue to attack them.

I recommend a whole-body approach to the warrior mindset. This includes mental health as well as physical fitness. If you need help, get it. There is no virtue in going it alone and pretending all is well when it clearly isn't. American soldiers were once taught that mental distress was a sign of weakness. No more. Now we are trained to recognize stress-induced symptoms and malaise in ourselves as well as others. We are encouraged and indeed commanded to weed out and deal with these issues using military medical care and veterans' assistance programs. It is implicitly understood that the American soldier must take his health seriously in every way and strive for complete perfection in mind, body, and spirit. No weakness is left unattended. Gyms are found on every base, and mental professionals are found in every base hospital. To fully embrace the warrior mindset, you must emulate the American soldier. You must recognize weakness, deal with it, and elevate your mind and body to new heights of physical achievement and peak mental strength. These are essential steps in building your warrior mindset.

The average American soldier of the 1940s was a hard man, likely raised on a farm and hailing from a family that had seen struggle and squalor. The Great Depression left almost no one untouched. That soldier probably spent his youthful years listening to combat tales spun by his father and grandfathers touching upon every important conflict from the Civil War to World War I. He was lean, tan, and tough-minded. He was a working man with a backbone, patriotism, and a sense of pride in himself. He had likely learned a little Latin, practiced fine cursive handwriting, and had a fair mastery of mathematics. That soldier and others like him from Kansas wheat fields, the deep hot South, and the Texas oil flats would go on to roll right over the vastly powerful and technologically advanced German Wehrmacht. That soldier and his buddies would turn back the Japanese onslaught and defeat the ferocious Imperial Army in hand-to-hand combat on remote volcanic beaches in the South Pacific.

The men and women who sacrificed life and limb to achieve these miracles are held in awe by present-day Americans who call them "The Greatest Generation." They deserve the title. They fought and died to earn it. The warrior spirit of that generation is unparalleled and unmatched even today. But I will say this about the modern American soldier: His tough attitude, fighting intensity, and know-how matches and, in some cases, exceeds that of his forefathers. Most American enemies will readily testify that the last warrior they want to meet on an open battlefield is a well-armed and angry American. Backed by terrifying technology and incorporating lessons learned in far-flung jungles and the mountains of Afghanistan, he is a consummate and exceedingly professional soldier who deals in punishment and aims to destroy, not pacify, his enemy.

This new soldier has the advantages of superior weaponry, sophisticated training, and advanced Western medical care. He has the resources and support of a powerful nation at his back. But above all else, he is imbued from day one of his training with the warrior mindset. He will enter combat for the first time with a clear mental edge and an unshakable belief in his self-sufficiency. He will do battle with the advantage of preordered and well-practiced objectives. If the enemy performs a certain action, then his response will be calculated to match, counter, and overwhelm it. No soldier on the face of the Earth can equal an American warrior's skill in battle, diversity in tactics, and brute determination—not an Afghani mountain goat, a Chinese PLA grunt, an Israeli commando, or even a Russian Spetsnaz trooper. If you ask, we'll bring it. We'll come down on you with ruthless force, and we won't stop until we crush you completely. It's what we do.

What we bring to the field in terms of equipment isn't what matters. Our special operations forces are capable of carrying out devastating operations in remote areas with virtually no support. Attitude is what defines the American soldier. First and foremost, the warrior spirit and a battle-ready ethos are our constant companions in battle. These are qualities that you can study, master, and carry into daily life to ensure success and survival, whether you face confrontations in a high boardroom or down at street level.

As noted previously, you must be prepared to act at a moment's notice. Crises are not generally slow-moving affairs. They happen suddenly, and your response time will be limited. Time and space will be compressed to such an extent that a few seconds will determine whether you will live or die. You have a lot to do in those precious seconds. Be prepared to react.

Any veteran of modern combat will tell you that no plan occurs as originally envisioned. Al-Qaeda ambushers attacking American patrols and convoys are generally unsuccessful, and they die. They might surprise a team, but the vast array of tactics and responses rolled out by the surviving soldiers are overwhelming to the average sniper or rocket team. The attackers run or die on the spot in each and every case.

Preparation is key. People who are unprepared to fight through a diverse array of scenarios die. Preparation is critical to your survival. Rehearse your actions in given situations. Be aware of your environment and potential threats. Carry your keys in your hand when crossing a dark parking lot, and be prepared to sprint to safety if approached by a stranger. Lock your doors and windows at night. Practice egress in the event of a fire. Run through the list of options in your mind that you can bring to bear in the event of a physical confrontation. Do these things well in advance. Do them regularly. The time to consider your options isn't when the gun is pointed at your head.

You must have a variety of practiced actions at your fingertips when a crisis boils over and you find yourself engaged in a conflict. You must remain calm and act rationally. Perform the actions you've rehearsed in their proper sequence, and you are much likelier to succeed and prevail, just as American soldiers do in chaotic and unexpected combat conditions.

Believing in yourself and your ability to accomplish a task is a critical component of the warrior mindset. Confidence is not an easy thing to come by. Even if you have it, there is a definite gap between believing and doing. Believing you can throw a slider is very different from doing it. The art of pitching consists of both belief in oneself and continuous practice. See where I'm going with this? I'm joining belief to rehearsing action as discussed above. Practice makes you confident. Confidence increases your chances of success in a stressful endeavor. These qualities build upon one another.

You can also improve confidence by utilizing a technique called "positive visualization." Imagining yourself performing a task and then physically practicing it builds a bridge between your mind and muscles. Boxers spar without opponents to build muscle memory. Actors rehearse lines and hit their marks well before filming begins. Believe in yourself and see yourself succeeding. Psychologists have confirmed that there is a very real connection between belief and successful action. If you believe you're going to win, you are much more likely to do so.

To recap, the combination of preparation and belief in oneself are the touchstones and essential foundation of the warrior mindset.

Master these concepts and you will be able to tap into and utilize the warrior ethos in everyday life to accomplish an innumerable variety of tasks and ensure victory in any serious conflict.

> "Victory at all costs, victory in spite of all terror, victory however long and hard the road may be; for without victory, there is no survival."
>
> —WINSTON CHURCHILL

FACTORS THAT DEGRADE THE WARRIOR MINDSET

Cultivating the warrior mindset isn't enough to ensure success. The fighting tool described in this chapter is certainly powerful. But like any other, it will fail you in the moment of most urgent need if not cared for properly. As oxidation dulls and pits metal, as dirt and grease foul high-tech rifles, and corrosion erodes electronic components, the warrior mindset can fall prey to a host of conditions that will blunt its fine edge. These include but are not limited to the list below:

- Inadequate physical condition
- Unmanaged anxiety
- Lack of preparation
- Poor situational awareness
- A negative mental state

Note that all these factors are precisely the reverse of those described earlier, the aspects most useful in building and maintaining the warrior mindset. Neglecting these or completely ignoring any one of them will hurt you in the long run and damage your chances of success.

Maintaining physical fitness is crucial not only to your health but also to your state of mind. A healthy mind is necessary in order to maintain the warrior mentality. You don't have to bench press 450 pounds or run a four-minute mile to be fit. Shedding the extra pounds and getting your body fat in line and your cholesterol under control do require extra effort, particularly if you've let these things slide and you're advancing in age. Still, you'd be amazed at what even a modest fitness program can do for you in a short period of time.

It's no secret that I love a good workout. My workout regimen is brutally harsh when compared to most physical fitness regimens. It's way over the top. I lift five days a week, swim three of those, and do Mixed Martial Arts three days a week. In addition, I hit the range and shoot at least eight times a month. I find this schedule enjoyable and rewarding. I'm aware that most people would view this as pure punishment and that hardly anyone would deliberately choose the lifestyle I've adopted, not without a gun to their head anyway. Yet the physical stressors and enhanced endurance I've experienced all contribute to and improve my warrior mindset. I face grueling challenges on a regular basis in order to earn a living. I've found a system that works for me. Whether you consult a trainer or design your own routine, you need to adhere to a fitness regimen. Again, physical fitness is vital to maintaining the warrior mindset.

Anxiety and unmanaged stress are pure killers. You must remain calm. You must have a positive outlook no matter the situation. An attitude of "I can" versus "I'm going to die" is always preferable. As it does with most negative emotions, your body banks anxiety. No one really understands why. Anger, regret, and hatred tend to stick with you, while joy and love are fleeting. Stash enough bad stuff down deep in your system and you'll erupt in all sorts of ways at some point down the line. You'll boil over when the situation is dangerous and you absolutely need a clear head. Trust me, I've seen it happen over and over.

At the slightest provocation, people detonate and say and do things they'll later regret. In hindsight, most find it difficult to reconcile their actions with their own self-image. The buildup of stress in their bodies and minds clouds everything they do and makes maintaining a warrior mindset impossible.

If you enter high-stress combat with a body and mind already stretched to the limit, you will probably perish. If you permit fear to own you, then you'll never find your way out of the woods and you'll die of exposure on some godforsaken hillside. If you allow your anger to overflow, then you'll lose any advantage you might have during critical, high-stakes negotiations in the boardroom.

Step back. Calm yourself. Learn and practice deep-breathing techniques. Mastering anxiety and fear and releasing stress are crucial to your well-being and ultimate success. Again, I recommend seeing a specialist in the event that your anxiety is unmanageable. Practicing and learning self-control will benefit you endlessly.

Stress will kill you. Remaining calm will save your life.

EPILOGUE

THE FINAL ASSESSMENT

EXFIL

I HOPE YOU'VE ENJOYED what you read here. The idea of combining my life experiences with a nontraditional survival manual chock-full of usable real-life tips is a unique one for me. I had not considered this dual-book concept when I set out to build a work based on my life in the field and at home. I'm sure you'll let me know how this works for you. I fully expect to hear from you on social media, in email, and in the forums. If you have criticism, be professional about it and tell me in a polite way. Nobody likes an asshole. I love constructive criticism. That's how we grow as human beings.

If you've absorbed what I've written and reached this section, you have undoubtedly gained some insight into the psychology of a warrior. You now understand what a mindset is and how best to turn it into a powerful weapon. I have given you more than one example of the battle-ready ethos in action. I have bulletized specific episodes from my life, most in order to make a point. Writing these things was a highly emotional experience, and I have been deeply moved by this recounting. Many days I did not look forward to the work because it was difficult to look back on a life that seemed to be full of failures and disasters. But I am nothing if not disciplined. *Lone Operator* is the end result of an attitude that I have worked hard to cultivate and one baked into me in the field. I get things done.

I have instructed you quite clearly in how to put that attitude to work for you. I have provided a list of factors that degrade a successful mindset and explained how best to avoid them.

I've even thrown in a bit of ancient and personal history to make my case. This book was formulated to provide information in a convenient and readable manner. There are no tests. There will be no pop quiz, oral or written, on the material covered. What you do with the information I've provided here is up to you. My hope is that you will set forth from this moment on a path of positive change and that you will build a mindset capable of seeing you through any adversity, a warrior mindset.

I hope you enjoyed *Lone Operator*. I have many interesting stories to tell, and there may very well be another book in the pipeline.

May God bless you.

CPSIA information can be obtained
at www.ICGtesting.com
Printed in the USA
LVHW111819270420
654541LV00008B/1590